Other Titles in the Crowood AutoClassics Series

PORSCHE
924 · 928 · 944 · 968

David Vivian

First published in 1993 by
The Crowood Press Ltd
Ramsbury, Marlborough
Wiltshire SN8 2HR

British Library Cataloguing-in-Publication Data

A catalogue record for this book is available from the British
Library.

ISBN   1 85223 483 0

Picture Credits

The majority of the photographs were supplied by the National
Motor Museum, Beaulieu, and Porsche Cars GB Ltd.
Artworks by Bob Constant.

Typeset by Chippendale Type Ltd, Otley, West Yorkshire.
Printed and bound in Great Britain by BPCC Hazell Books Ltd,
Aylesbury

Contents

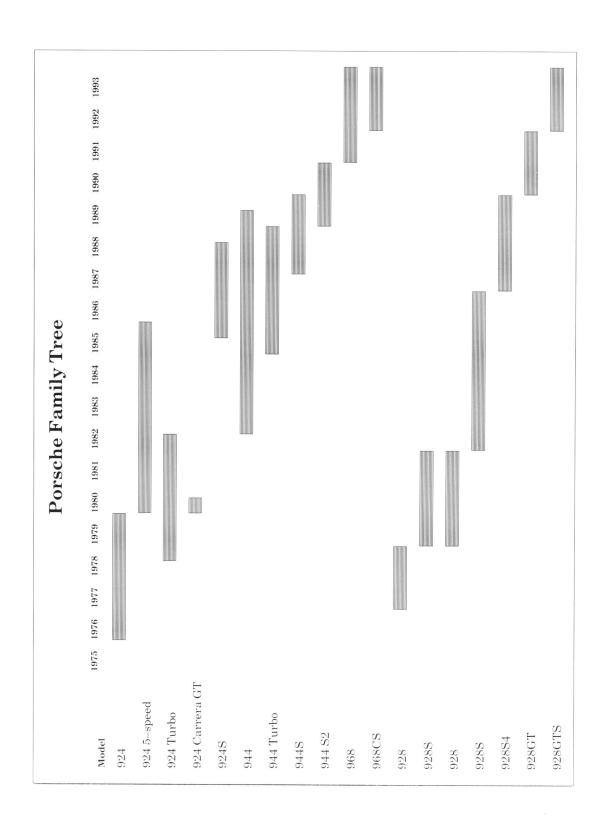

Porsche Family Tree

Introduction

Dr Ferdinand Porsche was born in 1875 in the Bohemian village of Maffersdorf. His father was the village tinsmith. His early career teamed him with Jacob Lohner in the production of an electric car before being invited to join the Austrian branch of the German Daimler Company, which later became Austro-Daimler, where he oversaw the development of the Prince Henry model, in particular the aerodynamics of its bodywork. He improved the car's speed by reducing its air resistance with the famous 'tulip form' shape. In 1923, Porsche joined Daimler in Stuttgart as Technical Director. He designed many successful models, none more impressive than the 250bhp SSKL.

His instinct was to develop a smaller, lighter car but this did not fit in with Daimler's plans. So, in 1929, he returned to Austria and joined Steyr. The timing could hardly have been worse for in the following year the Bodenkreditanstalt bank collapsed and, among other small companies, took Steyr with it. But this merely precipitated the inevitable. With some money borrowed from German racing enthusiast Adolf Rosenberger, Dr Porsche set up his own independent engineering design business in a small office in Stuttgart.

Dr Porsche employed a team of twelve engineers, including son Ferry and old friends Karl Rabe and Erwin Komenda. Rabe worked closely with Porsche thereafter, valued as much for his amicable Austrian outlook as his first rate technical brain. Komenda was another stalwart, chief of body design and the man responsible for the Beetle's body and that of the 356. He was a modest and self-effacing man but a

Ferdinand Porsche: 1875–1951.

progressive thinker. The company was called Dr Ing hc Ferdinand Porsche GmbH. Motorsport kept the company ticking over but its first milestone car was the VW Beetle, a car which provided the guiding principles for the first production Porsche, the 356.

At the end of the war, Dr Porsche – now over 70 and in poor health – was imprisoned by the French for nearly two years but survived the ordeal and, in 1948, rejoined his family in Stuttgart where son Ferry had re-kindled the family business and built a prototype that would become the 356. He had this to say about his new project: 'From the beginning we envisaged a small sportscar with which you could cover long distances without tiring the driver and co-driver. This idea couldn't be exploited because it didn't fit in with the national policy of the time. Three years after moving to Gmund in 1944, drawings were made for a sportscar based on the VW Beetle. The greatest part of our equipment had been lost in the war. Hardly any financial means were at hand, yet we were able to produce 50 high quality cars in the twelve months between 1948 and 1949. All were handmade, reflecting the quality for which we were soon to become world renowned.'

BIRTH OF THE 356

The 356 was based on the design of a special aerodynamic coupé built around the VW chassis and mechanicals. Three were made to compete in the Berlin to Rome road race but the outbreak of war scuppered the event. After the war, Ferry Porsche and Karl Rabe adapted the design to make a mid-engined, two-seater roadster which performed encouragingly in trials. As the car was developed, Erwin Komenda styled a body and the rear-engined 356 was born. It had an 1,100cc flat-four engine developing just 44bhp, but was capable of 80mph (129km/h) thanks to its low weight and aerodynamic shape.

In 1953, Porsche the car was joined by Porsche the badge. What has become one of the most distinctive emblems in motoring was designed by Max Hoffman, the sole US importer for Porsche during the 1950s and something of a marketing guru. Legend has it he sketched the basic design for the heraldic 'shield' on a napkin over lunch with Ferry Porsche in a New York restaurant. The final creation married the coats of arms of Baden–Wurttemberg and Stuttgart and initially, at least, was played down to such

Ferry Porsche aged 75. He was born on 19th September, 1909.

an extent that it wasn't placed on the outside at all and, on the inside, only in the centre of the steering wheel boss.

Production of the 356 spanned 17 years, from 1948 to 1965. In that time, engine capacity climbed from 1.1 litres to 2.2 litres and power from 40bhp to the 130bhp of the Carrera. The basic design was straightforward – a steel floorpan with welded box-section sills and a central tunnel, not, of course, to house the propshaft but for extra rigidity. The first 50 cars were handbuilt but when business moved back to Stuttgart in 1950, the need to boost the rate of production was solved by sub-contracting production of bodies to the firm Reutter Karosserie.

The 356's rear-mounted engine was essentially VW Beetle by Porsche, the familiar flat-four design receiving cylinder head and carburation modifications from the engineers at Zuffenhausen and driving the rear wheels via a non-syncromesh VW four-speed gearbox. The independent suspension featured parallel trailing arms at the front and swing axles at the rear supported on flexible trailing arms. Transverse torsion bars provided the springing with telescopic dampers at the front and the lever arm type at the back. Brakes were initially mechanically operated drums all round but soon changed to hydraulic operation and eventually to all-wheel discs.

By 1951, 356 production had risen to 60 cars a month and the 1000th Porsche was made at the end of August. There were several minor bodywork changes but more significantly it was now made out of steel for ease of production. Also in 1951 a bored-out 1,300cc version of the original unit was introduced developing 44bhp but, later the same year, this was upstaged by a re-designed 1,500cc unit with low-friction roller bearings, aluminium cylinder heads and larger Solex carburettors. Power leapt to 60bhp and top speed to 96mph (154km/h). Beefier brakes became part of the specification and telescopic dampers replaced the lever arm units at the back.

Changes for 1952 included the introduction of a new, all-synchromesh gearbox, a one-piece windscreen, the addition of a rev counter, fuel gauge and clock to the facia and the option of a radio. This was also the year the Hoffman-designed Porsche badge made its first appearance. All of this generated appropriate praise but could not divert attention from handling which, at best, was being described by motoring writers as 'challenging' and, at worst, as 'very tricky', especially in the hands of the inexperienced. The criticisms were not lost on Porsche who, the following year, instructed its salesmen to urge customers to become fully accustomed to their new cars over a few thousand miles before driving them hard. A positive Porsche initiative to improve the somewhat ponderous handling was still a few years away. Meanwhile, Porsche improved the refinement of the 356 with more soundproofing and a roller-bearing version of the 1,300cc engine. In March 1954, total production had risen to 5,000.

This was the year the 70bhp 1500S was introduced. It had a top speed of 105mph (168km/h) and accelerated from rest to 60mph (96km/h) in around 10 seconds. The following year, Porsche started to make the 356 a better handling car by giving the front suspension an anti-roll bar. And so the 356 evolved as the 356A in 1956 with further modifications to the engines, suspension and facia. A comprehensive redesign marked the launch of the 356B in 1960 and smaller (15in) wheels, fatter tyres and numerous chassis modifications softened the ride and improved the handling for 1962, the year the 1,500cc engines were enlarged to 1,600cc. More Bs were sold than any other 356 – over 30,000 were built during its four-year production run.

A final version of the 356, the C, was unveiled halfway through 1963. Cosmetically, it was very similar to the B: tell-tale signs were the larger rear window and redesigned road wheels and hubcaps. The latter was necessary to allow the adoption of disc brakes on all four wheels, the icing on a dynamic cake now far more appetising than that offered by the early cars. Engine options had been rationalized to two, 1600C and 1600SC, developments of the 1600S and Super 90. The 356 reached the end of the road in 1965, 15 years and 76,000 cars on, a total built around a core of coupés but including the Carrera, Cabriolet and Speedster models. Today, any 356 is a sought after classic. Then, it established Porsche as a world-class player on the sports car scene and made the company solvent enough to embark on its greatest adventure – the 911 – and all the cars that followed. Including the 924.

1 924: A New Beginning

The 924 revived an idea Porsche had not used since the 356 – to produce a car with enthusiast appeal from run-of-the-mill parts at an affordable price. In this case Porsche made its selection from the VW–Audi components bins, choosing an engine from one, a suspension from another and so on. But the 924 was significant for another reason – as the first of a new generation of front-engined, water-cooled models that would soon unleash the V8-engined 928 and see the 924 evolve into the 944 and, eventually, the 968.

BACKGROUND

Planning for the 'poor man's Porsche' started in 1972. By this time, VW–Audi was already committed to water-cooled, front-mounted engines and front wheel drive. Porsche investigated fwd as well but was unhappy with the ultimate handling characteristics: it limited the driver's choices. Nor would the new model have a live rear axle instead of independent rear suspension – there was a crucial difference between containing costs and risking a reputation. A

Objects of love and derision. Enthusiasts didn't want the 924 to muscle-in on the 911's act.

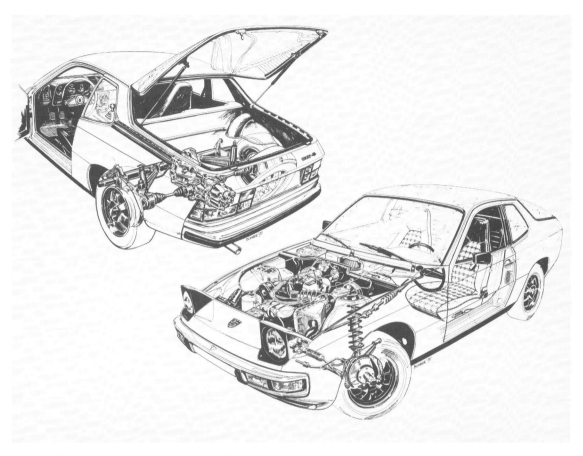

Despite the relative mundanity of its Audi-derived engine, the 924 (announced in 1975) was as elegantly engineered under the skin as it was pretty to look at. The MacPherson strut front suspension is from VW–Audi parts bin but the space-efficient transverse torsion bar rear suspension is more indicative of Porsche ingenuity.

rear-mounted transmission was chosen: first, it made the weight distribution more even, second it improved traction and, third, it gave a high polar moment of inertia allowing greater controllability in the event of a slide. Porsche's engineers were nevertheless keen that this did not sacrifice agility. And it was intrinsically interesting, a feature no rivals had. Given the otherwise quite mundane nature of the 924's design, the trans-axle added a little sparkle and distinction. It became the signature of the new front-engined Porsches.

At this stage, however, Porsche's engineers did not realize that they were playing through various chassis layout scenarios they would later have to act upon. Porsche had been asked to investigate the viability of a 924 by VW–Audi who wanted a flagship sports coupé for themselves. But the energy crisis and economic depression of the early 1970s forced them to reconsider and subsequently drop their production plans – or rather, hand them over to Porsche. The configuration eventually chosen reflected a mixture of inventiveness and pragmatism:

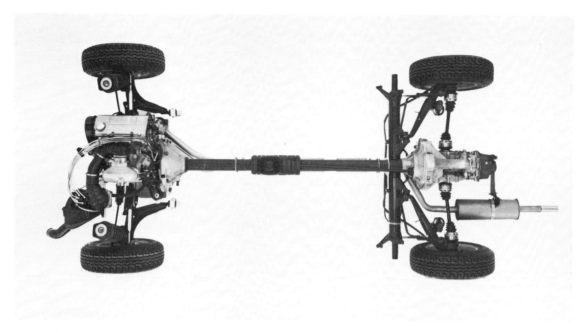

Porsche's transaxle transmission made its début with the 924 and would continue its career, in scaled-up form, on the 928.

front engine driving to the rear wheels via a transaxle. It had numerous advantages. First, the engine could sit behind the front axle line, giving a more even weight distribution front to rear (48/52 in unladen trim) and a reduced polar moment of inertia. Second, it provided weight over the driven wheels to aid traction.

Despite the cynics' cry that it was merely an up-market Audi, the 924 was very much its own car. The accusations were understandable all the same. Its engine and transaxle were from the Audi 100 and made by VW. And unlike the 356, which owed its existence to Ferry Porsche's love affair with sports cars, the 924 was the product of Porsche's growing adroitness at marketing. Indeed, it was the marketing department that drew up the brief for the 924. And the members of that department were working closely with those of VW for, since 1969, the two companies had been harnessed together

in the VW–Porsche Vertriebsgesellschaft (VG), an alliance struck up to make sports cars out of VW components. Its first product was the mid-engined 914.

DESIGN AND TESTING

By the time the 924 testing programme was under way, it had already been decided that a VW engine would power the car – one that itself was in its early development stages at the Audi Research Centre at Ingolstadt. Code-named EA831, it was an extensively developed version of the four-cylinder engine that had been introduced in 1965. To this end, it gained single overhead camshaft valve operation and a bore enlarged from 84 to 86.5mm which, with the 84.4mm stroke, increased the engine's displacement to 1,984cc. Bore centre distances were left unchanged at 95mm and, at 144mm, so was the length of the connecting rods: no modifications were needed for the block tooling. This unit would also end up in the VW LT van and the 1977 Audi 100.

Perhaps surprisingly in view of the onerous connotations, Porsche used the LT's single, belt-driven cam cylinder head virtually as supplied. With a higher, 9.3:1, compression ratio and Bosch K-Jetronic fuel injection, the engine nevertheless developed a respectable 125bhp (DIN) at 5,800rpm and 121.4lb ft of torque at 3,500rpm. Interestingly, Porsche could have used Bosch's more sophisticated L-Jetronic injection system but decided to go with 'K' because it was largely mechanical and therefore easier to service by non-specialist mechanics.

For the 924, however, the engine had both larger main bearings and a forged steel crankshaft. Also necessary was a special diecast sump since, for the Porsche application, the engine would be canted over to keep the 924's bonnet line low. Deep fins on the underside substituted for a separate oil cooler. The oil pump was a new crescent-type design circling the nose of the crankshaft, and the camshaft ran in five bearings in an alloy head, operating two valves per cylinder. Flat-topped cup-type tappets were used and a tapered side screw allowed easy adjustment. The distributor was mounted at the rear of the camshaft from which it took its drive.

A compact, inverted V-belt in front of the camshaft drive took care of the water pump

The limited edition 924 for 1977, with Martini livery. It didn't do much for the front-engined car's basic image problem.

924 (1976/77)

Engine
Longitudinal, front, rear-wheel drive

Capacity	1,984cc, 4-cyl in-line
Bore/Stroke	86/84mm
Compression ratio	9.3:1
Head/Block	Al alloy/Al alloy
Valve gear	Sohc, 2 valves per cylinder
Fuel and Ignition	Electronic ignition, Bosch Motronic K-Jetronic fuel injection
Max Power	125bhp at 5,800rpm
Max Torque	121lb ft at 3,500rpm

Gearbox
Four-speed manual

Suspension

Front	Independent, single wishbones, MacPherson struts, coil springs, telescopic dampers, anti-roll bar
Rear	Independent, semi-trailing arms, transverse torsion bars, coil springs, telescopic dampers, anti-roll bar

Steering
Rack and pinion, 4.0 turns between locks

Brakes

Front	Solid discs
Rear	Drums
ABS	Not available

Wheels and Tyres
Pressed steel, 5.5×14in, 165 HR14 tyres

Dimensions

Length	166in (4,216mm)
Width	66.4in (1,687mm)
Height	50.0in (1,270mm)
Weight	2,380lb (1,080kg)

and alternator while the fuel pump was one of the few electric parts of the K-Jetronic injection hardware. An unusual feature was the shroud for the alternator to keep it protected from the spray of salted roads in winter, with a pipe to blow air onto it for cooling. Engine coolant was pumped to a radiator with a separate plastic header tank itself cooled by an electrically driven fan with automatic thermostatic control.

But if adapting an Audi engine for service in the 924 was relatively straightforward, designing a transaxle was a process fraught with problems. Perhaps unsurprisingly, Porsche acquired an Alfetta to see how Alfa Romeo tackled the job. It soon became apparent that an obstacle the Italian car marker had found impossible to surmount was that of providing a decent gearchange. Two things in particular militated against achieving one: the length of the linkage and, because with a transaxle the propeller shaft is revolving whenever the clutch is engaged, the inertia of the shaft itself which, in turn, made life tough for the syncromesh. Porsche's solution was nothing if not original and involved a 85mm (3.3in) diameter length of tube rigidly bolted to the engine and to the front of the transaxle at the rear. This tube effectively encased the propeller shaft, itself supported on four sealed-for-life bearings. By using the ball bearing system, both the diameter and the mass of the shaft could be significantly reduced. The transmission tube solution also allowed the complete drive unit to be treated as one assembly, thus making installation that much easier. In the final design, the propshaft tube was 85mm (3.3in) in diameter with walls 4mm (0.16in) thick. The propshaft itself was 20mm (0.79in) diameter and 1,702mm (67in) long. It was made from torsion bar quality steel and weighed just 10lb (4.5kg).

The rigid link between the engine and the transaxle at either end of the car also licked the gearchange problem. Because the transmission unit was constructed for bolting on to the back of an engine, it came with its own bell housing for the clutch. Clearly, this was surplus to requirements for the 924 which had an engine with its own bell housing at the other end of the car. The transaxle's housing nevertheless made an excellent mounting for the gearchange rod which was passed through it, improving the quality of the shift no end. And as a unit with the housing, the tube acted as a support for the exhaust system.

Although based on the Audi 100's unit, the 924's transaxle was so intensively developed, it almost amounted to a new design and could handle much more torque, a feature that was also to benefit the 1976 Audi 100. Unsurprisingly, the 924's gear ratios differed from the Audi's, adopting a higher 3.44 to 1 final drive ratio instead of 3.70. In pursuit of better low-speed acceleration with the higher axle ratio, the bottom two gears were lowered – 2nd from 1.94 to 2.12, 1st from 3.40 to 3.60.

Support for the engine came from two rear mountings only, the transmission tube providing support in the horizontal axis. At the rear, two fabricated brackets supported the transaxle. Apart from anything else, this was designed to be a safe layout, Porsche claiming that in the event of a crash, the engine would be less prone to penetrate the cabin because the energy of the impact would travel along the transmission tube to be absorbed by the transaxle as well. Deliberately limited clearance around the redundant bell housing at the transaxle end prevented it from being driven forward as the result of a rear impact.

Disadvantages? It needed a big transmission hump in the cabin, the transaxle impinged on boot space and the higher rotating inertia of the driveshaft put a heavy strain on the transmission's synchronizers. So much so that Porsche had to spray the cone surfaces with molybdenum to improve their grip.

CHASSIS

A veritable *pot pourri*, the 924's chassis used MacPherson struts from the VW Golf but with the strengthened lower arms from the Scirocco. Also starting life on VW's humble hatchback were the 924's rack and pinion steering and safety column. Rear suspension represented a clever implementation of VW

Pop-up headlamps are one of the 924's more distinctive features.

The rear of the 924 – unadorned by spoilers.

Original 924 alloys: not wide, not pretty.

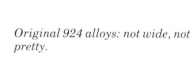

The exposed lockable petrol cap doesn't do much for the 924's appearance.

The 924's original facia design was later carried over to the 944. The instrumentation looks as if it belongs to a cheaper car.

Supplementary dials on the centre console contribute to the sporty look of the 924's cabin but they are hard to read at a glance.

The 924's seats look deceptively insubstantial but actually provide excellent support. The driving position in early cars was spoiled by the low steering wheel placement.

The 924's 'plus 2' rear seats are strictly for children. The tops of the backrests fold down to extend the luggage area.

Beetle parts with trailing links mounted to a transverse tube containing twin torsion bars. Jochen Freund's men developed anti-roll bars for the 924 – 20mm (0.79in) at the front, 18mm (0.71in) at the rear, though these were optional extras to begin with. Driveshafts? From VW's 181 all-terrain vehicle. Brakes? Discs at the front, drums at the rear – both courtesy of the VW K70. Servo assistance was standard and the hydraulic circuits split diagonally leaving one front and the opposite rear brake operational should something go wrong. And like the Golf, which donated its front suspension to the 924, the Porsche boasted outboard scrub radius geometry, giving a degree of automatic steering correction after a tyre blow-out or when braking on uneven grip surfaces.

All Porsche, however, was the 924's sleek and undeniably pretty body with its distinctively large wrap-around tailgate glass (*à la* Jensen Interceptor), integrated plastic bumpers and unusually clean detailing allowed, in part, by pop-up headlamps. Switching the sidelights on activated an electric motor which automatically raised the main units, even with the ignition switched off. In contrast to some of the outrageous claims made by manufacturers these days over the people-carrying ability of their 2+2s, Porsche never pretended that the 924 was anything other than a two-seater with a couple of cramped seats in the back suitable for children. And when the back seats were not in use, the top half of the rear backrest could be folded down to extend the depth of the luggage platform.

The neatly designed facia contained two instrument packs. The main display, clearly seen through the upper portion of the two-spoke steering wheel comprised a 155mph (250km/h) speedometer, a rev counter somewhat ambitiously red-lined at 6,500rpm and a composite dial containing gauges for coolant temperature and fuel level, and warning lights for battery, low fuel, oil pressure, handbrake and high temperature. All this was plainly presented and easy to read. Less successfully assimilated were the three gauges – oil pressure, oil temperature and a clock – sited down on the centre console. As for the rest of the cabin, it was deliberately and unmistakably Porsche: functionalism verging on the spartan with generous use of good quality black plastic – solid but not very sexy.

INTO PRODUCTION

Production started in 1976 in the old NSU plant at Neckarsulm, initially running at between 80 and 100 cars a day. The first batch of 'running improvements' came just over a year later. Most important was the

924 and its contemporaries

	cc	bhp	lb/ft	w/base	length	width	weight	mph/1,000rpm
Porsche 924	1,984	125	121	94.5	166	66.5	2,380	21.2
Alfa 2000 GTV	1,962	131	134	92.5	161	62	2,300	21.9
Datsun 260Z 2+2	2,565	150	158	102.5	174	65	2,630	22.6
Ford Capri GT	1,993	99	111	101	171	67	2,270	19.6
Lancia Monte Carlo	1,995	120	121	91	150	67	2,290	19.5
Lotus Esprit	1,973	156	140	96	165	73	2,015	21.7
Triumph TR7	1,998	92	115	85	164.5	66	2,241	17.9

introduction of a five-speed gearbox which allowed better spacing of the intermediate ratios. The unit was derived from that of the 911 and replaced the former Audi item, though a change to the final drive ratio (from the four-speeder's 3.444 to 4.714) kept the gearing in top the same with 21mph/1,000rpm.

With no change to the engine's outputs, any performance gains were never going to be startling but improvement was expected nonetheless When *Autocar* tested a Lux 5-speed in August 1978 it noted that first and second were both a little lower on the five-speeder, fourth a touch higher than the former's third. As for the performance, this is what the magazine's testers had to say:

The result is certainly that the 924 can be more readily kept at the top of its power band. It feels more lively and responsive to drive. The extra ratio neatly fills the previously wide gap between second (maximum 62mph) and third (98mph), having an 80mph maximum. Intermediate maxima in the five-speed box are 35, 56, 80 and 104mph. In purely straight line terms, the extra gear makes little difference. The two cars performed almost identically from standing starts, only showing slight differences caused by altered gearchange points. It reaches 60mph in 9.5sec, despite two gear-changes and pulls on to 100mph in 29.1 sec which is achievable in fourth. The improved driveability is hard to pin down on paper. The acceleration

Despite its van pedigree, the 924's 2-litre engine is a lusty workhorse.

figures in each gear show only the sort of small alterations that are compatible with the slight ratio changes, but the extra ratio does make a definite improvement to the 50–70mph time (6.0 sec instead of 7.1 sec) and 60–80mph (7.5 sec from 7.9 sec).

A 924 with real push, however, was only a matter of months away: the Turbo. Although, on the face of it, the new model seemed to be little more than the regular car with the addition of a blower and a few scoops and spoilers, it was rather more thorough than that. Porsche being Porsche, you wouldn't really have expected anything less.

ROAD TEST

Reproduced from *Motor*
12 February 1977

PORSCHE 924

With the introduction of the 924 in November 1975, Porsche history almost comes full circle. The very first car to bear this name was based on available mechanicals (those of the VW Beetle) which were clothed in a distinctive, aerodynamic lightweight body. Since then, of course, Porsches have come a long way – the only similarity between the magnificent Turbo and the original car, for instance, is the position of the horizontally opposed engine in the tail and air cooling.

Now, Porsche have reverted to using mass-produced parts in the 924, for it incorporates a high proportion of VW and Audi components: but in doing so they have broken with their mechanical tradition, for the 924 has an in-line water-cooled engine in the nose of the car and driving the back wheels.

In typical Porsche fashion, however, the car is not simple and straight-forward. When

Porsche first investigated the possibilities of the 924 (at the behest of VW, incidentally, who subsequently dropped their production plans which were promptly picked up by Porsche) they considered a number of layouts. There were no rear-engined models they could work from (Beetle production was being phased out), and the majority of the VW/Audi range was front wheel drive. They felt there would be traction problems with so much power through the front wheels, so their method of achieving rear wheel drive was simple and clever.

They took the Audi 100 engine/transmission unit which lies fore-and-aft in that model and split it between the clutch and the gearbox. The latter was moved to the rear axle complete with differential and the two parts were joined by a long tube within which runs the propellor shaft. They thus formed a rigid three-section drive train with a near ideal layout: front engine, rear transmission and drive. Another advantage is that it helps the weight distribution to come close to a 50/50 split, which Porsche claim helps with the handling (though the other models do remarkably well with a strong rearward bias) and leads to a higher polar moment of inertia which should give better directional stability and minimise twitchiness.

The engine chosen for the car is the 1984cc single ohc unit from the Audi 100, which in this application with Bosch K-jetronic fuel injection produces 125bhp (DIN) at 5800 rpm. The four-speed transmission also comes from the Audi, while the suspension is via MacPherson struts at the front and semi-trailing arms with transverse torsion bar springs at the rear. Steering is by rack and pinion, and the servo-assisted brakes use discs at the front and drums aft.

The sleek bodyshell is noteworthy in at least one respect: the whole of the bottom section, including the floorplan and wheel-arches, is made from galvanised steel, and with it goes an exceptional six-year guarantee provided that certain conditions are met (that it has not been involved in an accident, for example). Thus, though the 924 is cheaper than the other Porsche models, the company are determined that it will not be lacking in quality.

All this results in a car that has many traditional Porsche traits. The performance is excellent, especially considering the engine capacity, yet economy has not suffered. The handling is generally good (though with one or two odd quirks of behaviour) and the steering excellent. Passenger and luggage accommodation, however, is a bit cramped and the car is not as refined as we expected it to be – road noise in particular came in for criticism.

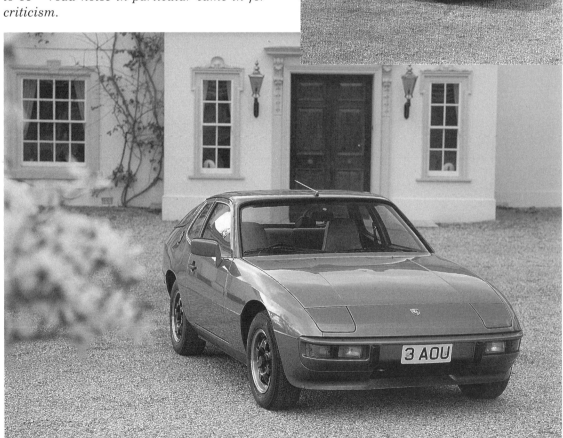

The 924's shape can not match the timeless quality of the 911's but it is wearing well. A Cd of 0.36 was a new low for production cars at the time of its launch.

The 924 is a sports car in the modern idiom, achieving much through efficiency rather than brute force: in this respect it is similar to the Lotus Eclat and Elite. But, like the Lotus twins, it is very expensive, especially considering the 'cooking' nature of the engine and the derivation of many of the mechanical components: at £7653 as tested it faces some stiff competition.

PERFORMANCE**

Audi's 1984 cc engine has a belt-driven overhead camshaft running in a light-alloy cylinder head. Equipped as it is in this application with the Bosch K-jetronic fuel injection system it produces 125bhp (DIN) at 5800rpm and 121.5lb ft (DIN) torque at 3500rpm.

At 20.2 cwt the 924 is relatively light which no doubt contributes to the excellent performance. It reached 60 mph from rest in a sharp 8.2s, less time than most of the competitors in our comparison chart. The only other 2-litre cars that come close to this figure are the Lotus Esprit (7.5s), Eclat (8.5s), Elite (7.8s), Triumph Dolomite Sprint (8.4s) and Ford's RS2000 (8.5s), all of which are very quick cars.

In addition a slippery shape and appropriate gearing give a high top speed of 121.3mph around MIRA's bank circuit, with a fastest quarter mile of 125mph. Knowing that tyre scrub on the bankings can have an effect at these sorts of speeds we see no reason to doubt Porsche's claim of a genuine 125mph under the right conditions. Whatever the figure, to achieve over 120mph from a 2-litre car is exceptional.

These figures rather surprised us, since on the road the 924 doesn't feel quite so quick, perhaps because of its high gearing which gives high maxima in the intermediate gears but comparatively poor top gear acceleration. If full performance is required then all the revs must be used. However at about 4000 rpm the engine starts to sound fussy, and at higher revs it becomes distinctly raucous and

there are some high-frequency vibrations transmitted through to the passenger compartment, which means that using all the revs is not very pleasant. For gentle driving, though, the engine is relatively unobtrusive, and cruising at the legal limit it is turning over at a restful 3400rpm.

Starting was instant, whatever the weather, and the engine settled down to a steady 800rpm without any apparent fast idle period, and would pull cleanly if not strongly from low revs before the water temperature gauge needle had moved from its stop.

ECONOMY***

One usual benefit of high gearing is good economy, and in this the Porsche runs true to form. We achieved 25.5 mpg overall, which compares well with other 2 litre saloons and coupes that don't go so fast and is better than the Lotuses (Eclat 19.5 mpg, Elite 21.7 mpg). Unfortunately we could not adapt our fuel measuring system to the injection set-up so could not record steady speed fuel consumptions and thus compute a touring figure. On more than one occasion we ran for about 300 miles and still had a couple of gallons in reserve in the tank, so we estimate the range to be about 350 miles – more with gentler driving.

TRANSMISSION**

Unlike the Alfetta, another car with a front engine and a rear trans-axle, the Porsche's clutch is mounted on the engine flywheel and is connected to the gearbox by a slim (20mm) shaft running in four bearings within the connecting tube. This not only reduces weight and whirling problems but also the loads on the synchromesh.

The clutch action is delightful, being silky and light: in conjunction with a progressive throttle this makes it easy to drive the 924 smoothly. The gearchange is also good, requiring just a flick of the light, short-travel, *precise lever for a quick change: however, reverse is too close to first, and the detents are not really strong enough to differentiate clearly between the two gears, so wrong slotting is too easy. Unlike that of the Alfetta, the synchromesh is unbeatable.*

All the ratios are high, top in particular, with maxima in the intermediates of 36, 62 and 96 mph which are comparable to those of the Eclat in the lowest three of its five speeds – but the better low-speed torque of the Lotus tends to mask this a little. The spacing of the ratios, however, is ideal. In spite of a high first gear ratio, the 924 coped easily with a restart on the 1-in-3 hill.

HANDLING***

The suspension of the 924 bears a family resemblance to that of the 911, with Mac-Pherson struts (but coil springs rather than torsion bars) at the front, and semi-trailing arms with transverse torsion bars at the back: the cross-tube which carries the arms also contains the torsion bars. Our test car was fitted with the optional anti-roll bars front and rear and alloy wheels shod with Dunlop SP 185/70 HR 14 tyres (normal wear is steel wheels and 165 HR 14 tyres). Like the Audi's, the front suspension has negative roll radius.

The steering of the 924 is very much like that of the 911, for it is light at anything above walking pace, and writhes gently in your hands, telling you exactly what the front wheels are doing: it is full of feel, precise and responsive – just as a good steering system should be.

In general the handling is also typically Porsche – it repays and rewards those who take pleasure in driving neatly and precisely, for it can be impressive – but it is not without faults to catch the unwary.

Up to moderately high cornering speeds it is nicely neutral and progressive, but on the limit it can be a little unpredictable. On tight corners it usually understeers quite strongly,

while on faster ones roll oversteer can develop and hence lead to a rather untidy line out of the corner. There is also strong lift-off lock-in, and a stint on a very wet steering pad showed that, after the initial tightening of the line, the nose can then break away.

The adhesion of the fat Dunlops was ample (as distinct from the exceptional grip of the 205/60 VR 14s as fitted to the Eclat 523 and the Elite) in the dry, but tended to deteriorate more than we liked in wet and/or greasy conditions.

Roll is well controlled, and only a strong sidewind had any noticeable effect on stability. Just over four turns from lock to lock may seem a lot, but in fact the turning circle is a very tight 29ft so the gearing is quite reasonable.

BRAKES****

The braking system is conventional, with discs at the front, drums at the rear, a servo and diagonally split circuits. This set-up is all that it should be: it pulls the car up all square, even with incipient locking (the negative roll radius probably plays a part here) and pedal pressures are light (at first they feel too light and overservoed, but you quickly adapt) and progressive. The handbrake achieved a very good maximum of 0.39g, and easily held the car facing either way on the 1 in 3 test hill.

ACCOMMODATION***

On paper the 924 is a sporting 2+2 hatchback. In practice space for rear seat passengers and luggage is pretty restricted. The major problem in the back is the lack of legroom, so that if two people even of average height are travelling one behind the other legroom is insufficient for both. There is plenty of headroom and width though. The back seats themselves are rather hard and small, too, so their use is effectively limited to children or for short journeys.

The luggage space is shallow and not very

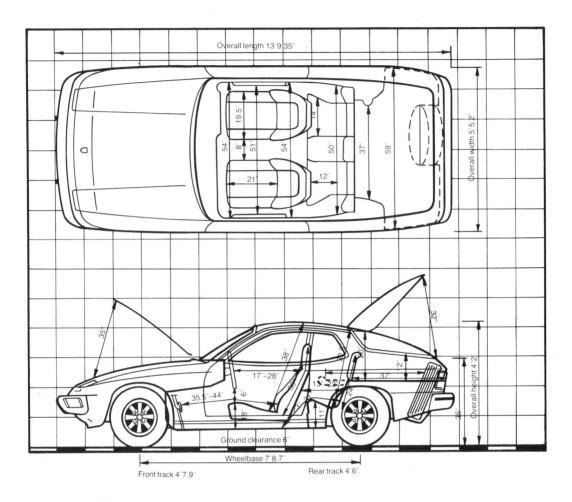

Overall length 13'9.35"

Overall width 5'5.2"

Overall height 4'2"

Ground clearance 6"

Wheelbase 7'8.7"

Front track 4'7.9"

Rear track 4'6"

Dimensions of the 924.

big. With the rear seat back-rest raised it took only 4.8 cu ft of our Revelation suitcases: even with it folded this only increased to 7.7 cu ft. In addition the rear window forms the boot lid, which means that there is a high lip over which luggage must be lifted. The spare wheel, stored upright against the rear panel also encroaches on valuable space.

Other than the main boot there are two pockets, hidden by wooden panels, in each rear wheel arch, an average-sized glove locker and smallish but useful bins under each armrest. All told, the 924 is a rather cramped car.

RIDE COMFORT***

On really bumpy roads the 924 absorbed potholes and the remnants of roadworks very well – but on smooth roads, motorways for example, it could at times be quite jerky and bouncy, while at low speeds even minor irregularities jarred the body. This is accentuated by poor bump-thump suppression which often makes matters feel worse than they actually are. Once again the 924 is typical Porsche in that the ride has to some extent been sacrificed for good, taut handling.

AT THE WHEEL***
Although cramped in the back, there is plenty of room in the front. Seat adjustment for reach is enormous (drivers of average height cannot reach the pedals with the seat right back) and the footwells are especially large, thanks to the rear-mounted gearbox.

The seats are from the 911, and very impressive they are too. They offer plenty of support in all the most important areas and, though firm, are very comfortable – everyone liked them.

With one exception, the layout of the major controls is very good. The stubby gearlever is a handspan away from the steering wheel, the handbrake is neatly placed to the right of the driver's seat, the pedals are laid out so you can heel and toe (though only just, as the accelerator is lower than the brakes). Our only complaint is that the slightly oval steering wheel is too low (or the seats too high) as your hands brush your thighs when turning a sharp corner.

The minor controls (which will look familiar to VW owners) follow modern practice in that most operations are carried out by two column-mounted stalks. That on the left works the indicators, and the flashers, that as the right takes care of the two-speed plus intermittent sweep wipers and washer. That leaves the light master switch on the bottom left corner of the instrument binnacle and the heated rear window and hazard warning switches on the bottom right. A little switch in front of the ashtray brings in the bumper-mounted driving lights, and the heater controls are in the centre of the console.

VISIBILITY***
Like many modern cars with wedge-shaped lines, the extremities of the 924 are invisible, though the rear window finishes quite close

the rear-most point of the tail. The tall passenger's seat headrest and rather thick three-quarter pillars also combine to create a blind spot at T-junctions; otherwise the view out is quite good. An exterior mirror is a standard fitting, but the wipers have not been converted to right hand drive, no rear wiper is fitted (it is an optional extra we think should be standard) and the rear window heater takes a long time to clear moisture from the glass. The lights are not especially powerful and the driving lights didn't seem to make much difference.

INSTRUMENTS****
The major instruments are contained in three large dials in a binnacle in front of the driver: that on the left is for the water temperature and fuel gauges, that in the centre is the speedometer and the tachometer is on the right. The conical glass covers are effective in preventing reflections, but the calibrations on the speedometer are rather sparse, with marks every 10 mph and numerals every 30 mph: in contrast the tachometer looks busy.

There are three other instruments on the centre console: an oil pressure gauge which in true Porsche tradition drops to zero when idling, a clock and a voltmeter. All the instruments are nicely lit at night.

HEATING***
The heating and ventilation system is operated by three straightforward slides in the centre console: the top one operates the fan (which is noisy at full boost) the middle one the temperature, and the bottom one the air direction. They work well but the symbols are too small (although owners would no doubt very soon get used to them without having to refer to the symbols). In general the system is adequate, except that heat takes a long time to come through on very cold mornings: once it is up to temperature, though, it provides a good supply of controllable heat.

VENTILATION****

There are four vents in the facia, two large ones in the centre and two smaller ones at each end. They can be fan boosted and thus provide a plentiful flow of cool air – which is no bad thing since ram pressure is not very strong. Each vent is finely adjustable for distribution and volume.

NOISE**

The 924's Achilles heel is that it's too noisy. As we mentioned, the engine is raucous and throbby at high revs which deters spirited driving. Wind noise (depending on external weather conditions) can also be obtrusive, and road noise – the worst offender of all – is loud. Some surfaces can set up an obtrusive roar, and even fine surfaces create some fuss, while cracks, cats-eyes, and other small irregularities result in considerable bump-thump. It is in this area – lack of refinement – that the 924 does not justify the £7650 price tag.

FINISH***

Those parts which Porsche make reflect the care and attention that is a Porsche hallmark. The paintwork is excellent, and panel fits are good. However, owners may not care for some minor items such as the switchgear which is lifted straight from the VW Golf. The gearlever knob came off, one of the heater slides stopped functioning perfectly, and it is necessary to line up the pins carefully in the tailgate with their respective orifices to ensure that it closes perfectly. Little things like this niggle on such an expensive car.

Aesthetically the interior is neat and smart, if perhaps a little too sombre in our example. The charcoal pin-stripe seat panels looked particularly fetching.

EQUIPMENT***

Again considering its price, we find the 924 rather sparsely equipped. Other models for the same or less offer such luxuries as a rear window wiper, a remotely adjustable external mirror, electric windows and a radio. It does, however, come with all the essential items of equipment plus a few luxuries such as the 911 seats, a tonneau cover which unfolds from the rear seat backrest, folding headlamps and extensive rust proofing.

IN SERVICE

We cannot see many owners of the 924 doing their own maintenance: for a start it is fitted with fuel injection which precludes tampering, and secondly the plugs look decidedly awkward to reach. However the other items requiring routine attention – the distributor, battery, reservoirs and air filter – are easy to get at. The heavy bonnet is opened by pulling a catch on the passenger's footwell, a stretch away from the driver.

Porsches only require servicing every 12000 miles, but they do need an oil change at 6000 miles (which we regard as a service). It is worth mentioning again here the full six-year guarantee given on the galvanised parts of the chassis, and the front wings are bolted, not welded on for quick replacement. It is interesting to note, too, that part panels for cheaper repairs are also being offered.

CONCLUSIONS

Without exception all our drivers thought the 924 was too expensive at over £7000 (you can get, for example, a Jaguar XJ4.2 Coupe for nearly the same price). But we all liked the car. It is a fine machine with many of Porsche's desirable characteristics – and a few familiar flaws, come to that. The nearest equivalents in the UK are the Lotuses, which are even more expensive, but considerably better equipped.

The 924 has many good qualities. The performance is very good, and all-out acceleration and top speed is nearly the equal of the Eclat or the Elite. The high gearing adversely effects top gear acceleration but it does give good fuel consumption taking the

PERFORMANCE

Performance tests carried out by Motor's staff at the Motor Industry Research Association proving ground, Lindley.

CONDITIONS
Weather	Cold, dry; wind 10–20mph
Temperature	36–38°F
Barometer	29.6 in Hg
Surface	Dry tarmacadam

MAXIMUM SPEEDS
	mph	kph
Banked circuit	121.3	195.2
Best ¼ mile	125.0	201.1
Terminal Speeds:		
at ¼ mile	87	140
at kilometre	108	174
Speed in gears (at 6500rpm)		
1st	36	58
2nd	62	100
3rd	96	154

ACCELERATION FROM REST
mph	sec	kph	sec
0–30	2.8	0–40	2.1
0–40	4.2	0–60	3.8
0–50	6.2	0–80	6.1
0–60	8.2	0–100	8.8
0–70	11.3	0–120	12.8
0–80	14.0	0–140	18.8
0–90	18.2	0–160	23.1
0–100	23.4		
0–110	34.3		
Standing ¼	17.0	Standing km	31.5

ACCELERATION IN TOP
mph	sec	kph	sec
20–40	11.4	40–60	7.3
30–50	10.3	60–80	6.0
40–60	10.0	80–100	6.1
50–70	10.0	100–120	6.3
60–80	10.3	120–140	7.3
70–90	11.7	140–160	9.7
80–100	14.3		

FUEL CONSUMPTION
Overall	25.5mpg / 11.1 litres/100km
Fuel grade	98 octane / 4 star rating
Tank capacity	16.4 galls / 62 litres
Max range	See text
Test distance	1223 miles / 1968km

BRAKES
Pedal pressure deceleration and stopping distance from 30mph (46kph)

lb	kg	g	ft	m
25	11	0.62	48	15
40	18	0.98	91	9
50	33	1.00±	30	9
Handbrake		0.39	77	23

FADE
20 ½g stops at 1 min intervals from speed midway between 40mph (64kph) and maximum (80.5mph, 129.5 kph)

	lb	kg
Pedal force at start	28	13
Pedal force at 10th stop	26	12
Pedal force at 20th stop	26	12

STEERING
Turning circle between kerbs
	ft	m
left	29.25	8.9
right	29.75	8.8
lock to lock	4.1 turns	
50ft diam circle	1.0 turns	

CLUTCH
	in	cm
Free pedal movement	0.6	1.3
Additional to disengage	2.5	6.4
Maximum pedal load	16lb	7kg

SPEEDOMETER (mph)
Speedo	30	40	50	60	70	80	90	100
True mph	27	37	48	58	66	75	85	95

WEIGHT
	cwt	kg
Unladen weight*	20.2	1026.2
Weight as tested	23.9	1214.2

*with fuel for approx 50 miles

GENERAL SPECIFICATION

ENGINE
Cylinders	4 in-line
Capacity	1984cc (121.06 cu in)
Bore/stroke	86.5/84.4mm (3.41/3.32in)
Cooling	Water
Block	Cast iron
Head	Light alloy
Valves	Sohc
Valve timing	
inlet opens	6° btdc
inlet closes	42° abdc
ex opens	47° bbdc
ex closes	2° atdc
Compression	9.3:1
Carburettor	Bosch K-Jetronic injection
Bearings	5 main
Fuel pump	Electric
Max power	125bhp (DIN) at 5800rpm
Max torque	121.5lb ft (DIN) at 3500rpm

TRANSMISSION
Type	4-speed manual
Clutch	Sdp, diaphragm spring
Internal ratios and mph/1000rpm	
Top	0.9667:1/20.8
3rd	1.36:1/14.8
2nd	2.125:1/9.5
1st	3.60:1/5.6
Rev	3.50:1
Final drive	3.444:1

BODY/CHASSIS
Construction	Unitary all steel
Protection	Main frame galvanised (6-year guarantee), Zinc-rich primer, electrophoretic dip, PVC undersealing, wax spray in cavities

SUSPENSION
Front	Independent by MacPherson struts; coil springs; lower wishbones; optional anti-roll bar
Rear	Independent by semitrailing arms; torsion bars; optional anti-roll bar

STEERING
Type	Rack and pinion
Assistance	None
Toe in	0° ± 5'
Camber	−20' ± 10'
Cestor	2° 45' ± 30'
Rear toe in	0° ± 10'

BRAKES
Type	Discs front, drums rear
Servo	Yes
Circuit	Dual
Rear valve	No
Adjustment	Manual on rear

WHEELS
Type	Alloy, 6J × 14
Tyres	Dunlop SP, 185/70 HR14
Pressures	25 psi F/R

ELECTRICAL
Battery	12V, 45Ah
Polarity	Negative
Generator	Alternator 75A
Fuses	18
Headlights	2×60/55W Halogen

IN SERVICE
Guarantee
Duration	12 months, unlimited mileage (chassis 6 year rust guarantee)

MAINTENANCE
Schedule	Every 12,000 miles
Free service	at 300–600 miles

DO-IT-YOURSELF
Sump	7 pints, SAE 30
Transaxle	4.5pints, SAE 90
Coolant	12.3 pints
Chassis lubrication	None
Dwell single	44°/55°
Spark plug type	Bosch W225T30
Spark plug gap	0.7mm
Tappets (cold)	0–10mm inlet / 0–40mm exhaust

Make: Porsche, Model: 924
Makers: Dr Ing h c F Porsche AG, Stuttgart-Zuffenhausen, West Germany
Concessionaires: Porsche Cars Great Britain Ltd, Falcon Works, London Road, Isleworth, Middlesex TW7 5AG, England
Price: £5,982 basic plus £498.50 car tax plus £618.44 equals £6,998.94. Extras fitted: metallic paint £290.49, stabiliser bars £80.73, stereo speakers, aerial and suppression £78.39, alloy wheels with 185/70 HR 14 tyres £284.42. Total as tested £7,652.97

***** excellent   **** good   *** average   ** poor   * bad

performance into account. Other plus points are the superb steering and brakes, the very comfortable seats, the delightful clutch and gearchange and the external finish.

We have reservations about some aspects of otherwise good handling; the accommodation (particularly legroom in the back and luggage space); a ride which errs on the firm side and most importantly, the high noise from the engine and suspension. On the whole, though, the good points outweigh the bad, and the 924 is in this respect at least a true Porsche.

924 TURBO

The iron block engine's capacity of 1,984cc remained the same. Indeed, the bottom end was deemed strong enough to cope with the extra action. Modifications elsewhere, however, were extensive. An all-new cylinder head (aluminium as before) had different combustion chambers, recessed valves, 3mm large exhaust valves, spark plugs with the silver electrodes moved across to the intake side and a compression ratio dropped from 9.3 to 7.5 to 1. The German-made KKK turbocharger was situated low down near the front under the lee of the heavily inclined engine, drawing air from the Bosch K-Jetronic flap valve box and air filter assembly mounted transversely across the front of the engine. It blew through a cast pipe into the inlet manifold, which turned the flow down and back into the ports on the upper side of the engine.

In a similar arrangement to that on the 911 Turbo, a wastegate was used to limit the boost of the exhaust-driven turbine and, to keep the throttle response sharp, a blow-off valve between the pressure and inlet sides of the inlet system relieved back pressure which would otherwise slow down the turbo when the throttle was momentarily closed. Fuelling remained by Bosch K-Jetronic

---

Porsche 924

The Porsche 924 was launched in Germany in 1975, breaking with Porsche tradition by having a front engine and rear-wheel drive. The model was first imported into Britain in March 1977 with four-speed manual or three-speed automatic transmission. Its specification was improved in September of the same year and a 'Lux' model introduced with alloy wheels, tinted glass and a rear wiper as standard equipment.

Special editions

A number of 'special edition' 924s were offered with 'designer' trim packages. These were:

Martini – 1976, all white bodywork, white alloy wheels, tapering Martini colours down the sides, black interior, red carpets, blue seat inserts, sunroof, four-speed gearbox. Only 100 were built.
Doubloon – 1979, pale gold metallic paint, polished black alloy wheels, tan pinstriped interior. Only 50 built.
Le Mans – 1981, white paintwork, German colours running around body, turbo-style wheels (four-stud), Pirelli P6 tyres, black seats with white piping, Koni dampers and anti-roll bars, turbo rear spoiler, sunroof, 924 Turbo steering wheel. Only 100 built.

---

mechanical injection but the system was made larger and recalibrated to cope with the higher outputs. The inevitably higher operating temperatures were tackled by an oil cooler and additional cooling vents in the nose of the car. All the extra engineering added some 220lb (100kg) to the 924's kerb weight, but this was comfortably offset by the 36 per cent hike in power – 170bhp against 125bhp – and, better still, a 48 per cent increase in peak torque, taking the figure to 181lb ft at 3,500rpm.

924 Turbo (1979)

Engine

Longitudinal, front, rear-wheel drive

Capacity	1,984cc, 4-cyl in-line
Bore/Stroke	86/84mm
Compression ratio	7.5:1 (8.5:1 Series 2, 1980–82)
Head/Block	Al alloy/Al alloy
Valve gear	Sohc, 2 valves per cylinder
Fuel and Ignition	Electronic ignition, Bosch K-Jetronic fuel injection. KKK turbocharger
Max Power	170bhp at 5,500rpm (177bhp/5,500rpm S2)
Max Torque	181lb ft at 3,500rpm (184bhp/3,500rpm S2)

Gearbox

Five-speed manual, auto not available

Suspension

Front	Independent, single wishbones, MacPherson struts, coil springs, telescopic dampers, anti-roll bar
Rear	Independent, semi-trailing arms, transverse torsion bars, coil springs, telescopic dampers, anti-roll bar

Steering

Rack and pinion

Brakes

Front	Ventilated discs
Rear	Ventilated discs
ABS	Not available

Wheels and Tyres

Cast alloy, 6×15in, 195/65 VR15 tyres (16in wheels with 50-series tyres introduced in 1982)

Dimensions

Length	167in (4,243mm)
Width	66.3in (1,687mm)
Height	50.0in (1,270mm)
Weight	2,380lb (1,080kg)

In turn, the diameter of the propshaft went up from 20 to 25mm (0.79 to 1in). Half shafts for the semi-trailing rear were strengthened, too, and the gearbox ratios altered marginally. The chassis underwent similar up-grading with stiffer springs, dampers and anti-roll bars and the bigger brakes – ventilated discs all round – acquired a more efficient servo. Larger tyres were fitted – 185/70 VR 15 Pirelli Cinturato

CN36 SMs on 6in rimmed cast alloy wheels – but British market cars did even better, sold with 205/55 Pirelli P7s on 16in rims as standard. Other chassis changes included lower-geared steering and slightly more positive offset for the front suspension geometry. Wheel bearings were stronger and the new alloy wheels had five instead of four stud fixings.

PERFORMANCE

The 924 Turbo's measured performance more than fulfilled the promise of its specification. In its 1980 road test of one of the first right-hand drive examples, *Motor* magazine achieved a top speed of 140mph (225km/h), 0–60mph (0–96km/h) in 7.0sec and 0–100mph (0–160km/h) in 17.9sec – very impressive figures more than a decade on. But tapping this Porsche's potential was not always a pleasure as the test explained:

Unfortunately, high gearing exaggerates an acknowledged turbocharged engine failing: lack of low speed pull. At low engine speeds, there isn't enough energy in the exhaust gases to produce significant turbo boost, and even Porsche haven't overcome this failing. Floor the 924 Turbo's throttle when travelling slowly in fifth, and the acceleration from 30 to 50mph takes a yawning 14.7sec. Compare that with

The 1980 Porsche 924 Carrera GT. Only 75 were imported to Britain.

924 Carrera GT (1980)

Engine
Longitudinal, front, rear-wheel drive

Capacity	1,984cc, 4-cyl in-line
Bore/Stroke	86/84mm
Compression ratio	8.5:1 (8.0:1 GTS, 7.0:1 GTR – both 1981)
Head/Block	Al alloy/Al alloy
Valve gear	Sohc, 2 valves per cylinder
Fuel and Ignition	Digital electronic ignition, Bosch K-Jetronic fuel injection (Kugelfischer GTR), KKK turbocharger, intercooler
Max Power	210bhp at 6,000rpm (245bhp/6,250rpm GTS, 375bhp/6,400rpm GTR)
Max Torque	206lb ft at 3,500rpm (247lb ft/3,000rpm GTS, 299lb ft/5,600rpm GTR)

Gearbox
Five-speed manual

Suspension

Front	Independent, single wishbones, MacPherson struts, coil springs, telescopic dampers, anti-roll bar
Rear	Independent, semi-trailing arms, transverse torsion bars, coil springs, telescopic dampers, anti-roll bar

Steering
Rack and pinion

Brakes

Front	Ventilated discs (cross-drilled GTR)
Rear	Ventilated discs (cross-drilled GTR)
ABS	Not available

Wheels and Tyres
Cast alloy, 7×15in, 215/60 VR15 tyres (7×16in front, 8×16in rear with 205/55 VR16 and 225/50 VR16 tyres GTS; 11×16in with 275/600×16 front and 300/625×16 rear racing Dunlop tyres)

Dimensions

Length	170in (4,318mm), 167in (4,243mm) GTS and GTR
Width	68.0in (1,727mm), 72.8in (1,849mm) GT and GTS
Height	50.0in (1,270mm)
Weight	2,602lb (1,180kg), 2,472lb (1,121kg) GTS, 2,084lb (945kg) GTR

the 70–90mph time in the same gear of 8.7sec, or the fourth gear times of 8.8sec (30–50mph) and 5.9sec (70–90).

Fast enough for most people you might have thought, but Porsche had other ideas. The Carrera GT took the 924 just about as far as it was possible to go in road car trim and commemorated the fact that, in 1980, Porsche had pushed the 924 to its limits on the track, taking 6th, 12th and 13th in the Le Mans 24-hour sportscar classic. A total of 400 production Carreras were built for homologation in Group B. Its basis was the regular all-steel body of the regular 924, onto which Porsche grafted the small rear spoiler of the Turbo and nose/flank body extensions made of polyurethane. The modified nose section reduced the Cd to a (then) very respectable 0.34 while the more bulbous wheelarches were needed to accommodate the 215/60 VR15 Pirelli P7s on 7J rims.

The Carrera used essentially the same engine as the Turbo, but with an intercooler to reduce the temperature of the intake air on its journey from the turbocharger to the engine which, in turn, allowed the compression ratio to be raised from 7.5 to 8.5:1 and boost pressure from 0.65 to 0.75bar. This was enough to increase power by 33bhp to 210bhp (DIN) at 6,000rpm and lift the peak torque figure from 181 to 203lb ft at 3,500rpm. To cope with the higher stresses, pistons were forged rather than cast and the tappet material up-graded. As tested by *Motor*, the figures reflected the fairly mild state of tune: 60mph (0–96km/h) came up in 6.5sec and 100mph (160km/h) in 16.7sec, respectively 0.5 and 1.2sec better than the straight Turbo's.

Meanwhile, the Turbo itself was undergoing a few minor modifications for 1981. The KKK turbo was replaced by a smaller unit with the object of giving better response and lowering the point at which it started to

Echoes of track success with the limited edition 924S Le Mans. But this 1988 version of 2.5-litre 160bhp Porsche was only cosmetically up-rated.

924S (1986)

Engine
Longitudinal, front, rear-wheel drive
Capacity	2,479cc, 4-cyl in-line
Bore/Stroke	100/79mm
Compression ratio	9.7:1
Head/Block	Al alloy/Al alloy
Valve gear	Sohc, 2 valves per cylinder
Fuel and Ignition	Electronic ignition, Bosch Motronic fuel injection and engine management
Max Power	150bhp at 5,800rpm
Max Torque	144lb ft at 3,000rpm

Gearbox
Five-speed manual or three-speed automatic

Suspension
Front	Independent, single wishbones, MacPherson struts, coil springs, telescopic dampers, anti-roll bar
Rear	Independent, semi-trailing arms, transverse torsion bars, coil springs, telescopic dampers, anti-roll bar

Steering
Rack and pinion, power assistance

Brakes
Front	Ventilated discs
Rear	Drums
ABS	Not available

Wheels and Tyres
Cast alloy, 6×15in, 195/65 VR15 tyres

Dimensions
Length	167in (4,243mm)
Width	66.3in (1,687mm)
Height	50.0in (1,270mm)
Weight	2,380lb (1,080kg)

provide effective boost. Compression ratio was raised from 7.5 to 8.5 to 1 and the former breakerless ignition replaced by a Siemens-Hartig digital system. These changes gained 7bhp, taking the peak output to 177bhp. Other detail changes included the addition of repeater flashers on the sides of the front wings, a change to white figures on the instruments and a new stalk on the steering column.

Ferry Porsche celebrates the production of the 100,000th 924 in 1981.

It was the 924S of 1985, however, that took the model to the end of the road. Initially powered by a de-tuned version of the Porsche-made 'balancer-shaft' 2.5-litre engine from the 944, it acquired the full-tune 160bhp unit and power steering as standard in 1987 and, with it, the kind of performance that plugged the gap left by the now defunct Turbo: 137mph (220km/h), 0–60mph (0–96km/h) in 7.4sec and 0–100mph (0–160km/h) in 20.1sec. I wrote the test for *Motor* and concluded that although Porsche's pricing policy did not do the 924S any favours, the car had stood the test of time:

The story here isn't so much about an extra 10bhp as perceived value. For what it offers, this car is too much money. A Mazda RX-7 does roughly the same job for around £6000 less. A BMW does a very much better job for around £2000 more. In a logical world, the 924S would be a non-starter.

Yet the 924S exploits the illogical. Crucially, it represents the first rung of the Porsche ladder and, to that extent, it can shrug off value judgements a little more easily than most. This is the best 924 yet.

It was also the last.

2 928: Following a Legend

If the 924 made people look at Porsche in a different light, the 928 must have made them think they were dreaming. Inasmuch as it was a 'supercar' like the 911, it fulfilled the crucial qualification but, for dyed-in-the-wool Porsche fanatics, its methodology was highly questionable. The front engine/transaxle layout that served the 924 was not good enough for a 'serious' Porsche, they argued. And a V8 engine? The stuff of Yankie muscle cars!

From Porsche's point of view, however, the 928 made perfect sense. Indeed, the company viewed it as the only logical way to go forwards. Here was a car that would buffer them from the repressive legislation that made the long-term viability of a rear-engined design look uncertain to say the least; a car with which to broaden their market aspirations, allowing them to take on Mercedes, BMW and Jaguar. Even, as fate would have it, a future Car of The Year. But the worry remained. With its front-mounted, 90 degree V8 driving the rear wheels via a transaxle, the 928 was a car not only far removed from the rear-engined, air-cooled flat-six concept of the 911, but the product of what many saw to be a compromised design philosophy which rejected the acknowledged dynamic benefits of a mid-engined layout for the 'soft option', a sop to user convenience and practicality.

So how do you follow a legend? As early as 1971, Porsche had realized that the 911 would not last forever and feared that it might not make it to the end of the decade.

The pessimism, as we now know, proved unnecessary but the urge to design a new car to keep the Porsche flag flying high when the 911 finally let go was irrepressible. What was to become the 928 – a superfast 2+2 GT in the mould of the Aston Martin V8 and Jaguar XJ-S – started with a clean sheet of paper and would be Porsche's first 'pure' design, no VW parts required – though Porsche's acquisition of Volkswagen's EA425 project (924) shortly after the serious work on the 928 commenced meant that both designs inevitably ended up with a common layout.

BASIC LAYOUT

The big decisions were quickly taken. The 928's basic layout would be designed to achieve, as near as possible, 50/50 weight distribution: front engine driving rear wheels with the gearbox (five-speed manual or three-speed auto) rear-mounted in-unit with the final drive. In the early 1970s, emissions legislation was becoming so tough, it looked as if air-cooled engines might be outlawed altogether, so Porsche designed a brand new water-cooled unit for its second generation flagship.

A V6 was considered – and well-liked on grounds of compactness and efficiency – but, in the end the design team plumped for a large capacity V8 which would achieve the performance targets with less effort and be well accepted in the potentially lucrative US

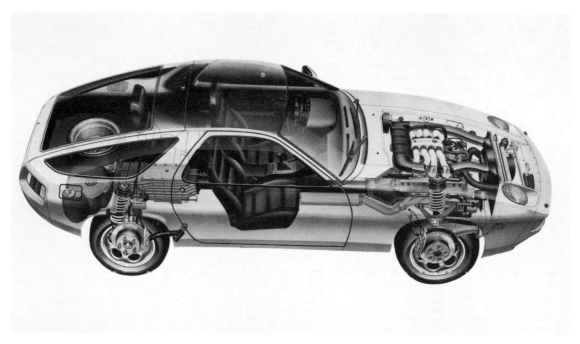

The 928 in cutaway – the classic high performance grand tourer.

The 928's transaxle layout mirrors that of the 924 and 944.

market. The distinctively bulbous styling was more of a gamble. Penned by Porsche's then head of design, an American called Tony Lapine, it clearly hailed from the same stable as the 924, but the bigger car's curvaceousness was much more boldly resolved, a feature enhanced by the apparent elimination of bumpers. In fact these were concealed by large, deformable body-colour panels at the front and rear. Also unusual were the pop-up headlights which were effectively front-hinged and therefore laid back into the wings when retracted *à la* Lamborghini Miura.

Striking in shape, the 928's body was also long-lasting and the mechanicals contained therein easy to service. The key to longevity was Porsche's extensive use of corrosion-resistant aluminium out of which the wheels, the doors, the bonnet, the transaxle housing, the front suspension wishbones, the rear suspension uprights, upper links and main crossmember and the cylinder heads, block and crankcase of the 4.5-litre V8 were made. The rest of the car was constructed either from galvanized steel or plastic. Servicing requirements were minimized because the engine had self-adjusting valves and contactless ignition, a long-life battery and oversized fuel and oil filters, stretching oil-change intervals to an almost unprecedented 12,500 miles (20,000km).

But then most things about the 928 were big, even by supercar standards. And the one external dimension that was not (an overall length of 14ft 7in (4,445mm), just 9in (229mm) longer than the very compact 911) only served to accentuate the car's dramatic width of just over 6ft (1,829mm). A kerb weight of around 3,200lb (1,452kg) might even have seemed excessive but for the balancing influence on the 4,474cc engine which countered with 240bhp at 5,500rpm and 257lb of torque at 3,600rpm.

ENGINE

Impressive and effective as these figures were, they were not the product of an engine being asked to work hard for its living. This ingenious new design would produce far bigger outputs in years to come because Porsche's engineers had done their homework thoroughly. Their all-alloy V8 was an unmistakably modern unit with a single overhead camshaft per cylinder bank operating in-line valves via hydraulic tappets and steel-coated aluminium from which the engine was made – a high-silicon alloy called Reynolds 390 – eliminated the need for steel liners.

Under the block (made from the same Reynolds alloy), an aluminium ladder frame combined all the five main bearing caps in a single, substantial casting. Wet sump lubrication was used and a crescent-type pressure pump and an oil/water heat exchanger formed a unit with the left hand header tank of the radiator. Other engines had used Bosch's K-Jetronic fuel injection by the time the 928 was launched in 1977, but the Porsche was the first car whose engine had been designed with it as a specific component. That is why the cleft of the engine 'vee' over the back six cylinder was left free to accommodate the duct that ushered air down from the injection metering unit.

Cylinder head design was more conventional and employed wedge-shaped combustion chambers. Cam-drive was by cogged rubber belt, the back of the belt turning the water pump at the front of the block. An additional aid to serviceability was the easy access to the spark plugs and injector nozzles, both located above the heads.

BRAKES AND SUSPENSION

The 928's high weight and power made an

The 928's V8 is a compact engine for its outputs.

exceptional braking system essential. And that is just what it had: large ventilated discs all round, 11.1in in diameter at the front, 11.4in at the rear – gripped by floating calipers. Twin, diagonally-split circuits and servo assistance were also part of the specification, but ABS would not come for a few years.

As advanced as anything on the market already, however, was the 928's racing-

---

928 (1977)

Engine

Longitudinal, front, rear-wheel drive

Capacity	4,474cc, 8-cyl in vee
Bore/Stroke	95/79mm
Compression ratio	8.5:1
Head/Block	Al alloy/Al alloy
Valve gear	Sohc, 2 valves per cylinder
Fuel and Ignition	Electronic ignition, Bosch K-Jetronic fuel injection
Max Power	240bhp at 5,500rpm
Max Torque	257lb ft at 3,600rpm

Gearbox

Five-speed manual

Suspension

Front	Independent, double wishbones, telescopic dampers with co-axial coil springs, anti-roll bar
Rear	Independent, lower wishbones, upper transverse link (Porsche–Weissach patent geometry), coil springs, telescopic dampers, anti-roll bar

Steering

Rack and pinion, power assistance

Brakes

Front	Ventilated discs
Rear	Ventilated discs
ABS	No

Wheels and Tyres

Cast alloy, 7.0×16in Pirelli P7, 225/50 VR16

Dimensions

Length	175in (4,445mm)
Width	72.3in (1,836mm)
Height	51.8in (1,316mm)
Weight	3,236lb (1,468kg)

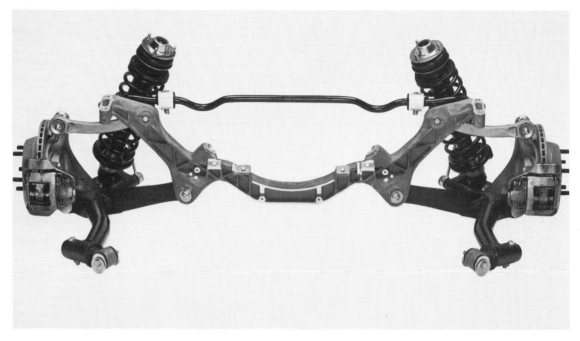

The 928's patented Weissach rear axle compensated for changes in toe-in during driving.

derived suspension. On the face of it, there was nothing unusual or innovative about using wishbones and coils front and rear but, for this car, it was the wealth of clever detail in its implementation that made all the difference. For starters, the front suspension geometry used negative scrub radius to give more stable braking when the car straddled surfaces with unequal grip. The rack and pinion steering had power assistance that lessened its servo effect with speed.

More subtle still, however, was the Porsche engineers' adaption of the rear suspension – essentially a simple lateral link and a wide-based lower steel wishbone – to provide both a degree of 'compliance steer' coupled with more progressive transient behaviour on the limit. Observing that rubber suspension bushings tend to let the rear wheels toe out under deceleration or braking – thereby creating instability and a propensity for the

car to swerve into a bend or 'lift-off over-steer' in modern road testing parlance – Porsche designed a special rubber-bushed link to go in the front joint of each lower wishbone and prevent the rear wheels from toeing out. This device was dubbed the 'Weissach Axle' to mark the achievement of the engineers at the Weissach Research and Development Centre who developed it. A suspension as thorough and well engineered as this deserved serious wheels and tyres and 225/50 section Pirelli P7 rubber on 16×7J cast alloy were about as good as they came in 1977.

RECEPTION

Technical *tour de force* as it was, however, the 928 was not as quick as the 911 and, indeed, failed to set any new standards for the GT class. As *Motor* said in its 1978 road

40

test: 'To accelerate from 0–60mph in 7.0sec and to 100mph in 17.8 sec makes the 928 no sluggard, but the Jaguar XJ-S, the Aston Martin V8 and the Ferrari 308 GT4 do it faster. In top gear, too, the 928 sets no new standards.' The 140mph (225km/h) top speed, while clearly more than adequate, was not quite in the Jaguar/Aston Martin/ Ferrari league, either.

The Porsche did not receive too much censure for its mildly uncompetitive showing against the clock, though. More important, the majority of critics felt, was the smoothness and lack of temperament with which the performance was delivered and the sheer docility of the car when trickling around in traffic. An overall fuel consumption of around 15mpg (18.9l/100km) was pretty reasonable, too, and the gearchange impressed by being fast and light, despite the initially awkward shift pattern with first out on a dog leg to the left. Comfortably the subject of most praise, however, was the way the 928 handled for such a big car. Always good at steering, Porsche's engineers had managed to endow the 928's power-assisted rack and pinion arrangement with meaty weighting and more sheer feel than many an unassisted system. Save for a slight lifelessness about the straight ahead position, the steering was precise and responsive as well, with plenty of bite when turning into a bend.

Unsurprisingly, the cornering forces that could be generated by those fat Pirelli P7s were prodigious but, even better, was what happened when the grip ran out – either in the wet or through generous applications of throttle in a low gear. Then the 50/50 weight distribution and anti-toe out Weissach Axle came into their own, refusing to let the chassis do anything hasty but, instead, ushering the cornering balance through a broad neutral phase before the onset of gentle, easily catchable oversteer.

Excellent stability at high speed also

Porsche 928 vs the class of 1978

Max speed: mph (km/h)

Aston Martin V8	146 (235)
Jaguar XJ–S	142 (228)
Porsche 911 Carrera 3.0	141 (227)
Porsche 928	138 (222)
Mercedes 450 SLC	136 (218)
Maserati Khamsin	130 (209)

Acceleration 0–60mph (0–96km/h) secs

Aston Martin V8	7.2
Porsche 911 Carrera 3.0	7.3
Jaguar XJ–S	7.5
Maserati Khamsin	7.5
Porsche 928	8.0
Mercedes 450 SLC	9.0

Overall mpg (l/100km)

Porsche 911 Carrera 3.0	21.0 (13.4)
Maserati Khamsin	15.1 (18.7)
Porsche 928	14.6 (19.3)
Mercedes 450 SLC	14.1 (20.0)
Jaguar XJ–S	14.0 (20.2)
Aston Martin V8	13.0 (21.7)

Size and Space:
Legroom front/rear in (cm)
(seats fully back)

Aston Martin V8	43/31 (109/78)
Mercedes 450 SLC	41/33 (104/83)
Jaguar XJ–S	42/30 (106/76)
Porsche 911 Carrera 3.0	43/28 (109/71)
Porsche 928	41/27 (104/68)
Maserati Khamsin	43/10 (109/25)

featured in the 928's extensive dynamic repertoire, backed up by strong and tireless brakes. Somewhat less wonderful, however, was a ride quality which *Motor* described as 'distinctly firm and restless at low speeds on small bumps, accompanied by a lot of bump thump'. Although the ride smoothed out to a degree at higher speeds, the 928 was no Jaguar when it came to smothering bumps, that much was clear.

ROAD TEST

Reproduced from *Autocar & Motor*
23 September 1992

PORSCHE 928 GTS

Extend the 928 GTS on a demanding road and you understand something important about the engineers at Porsche. They drive hard. Despite the impression that Zuffenhausen's celebrated grand tourer has been polished and preened and smoothed free of all rough edges for what many believe is its final, £64,998 incarnation, it's still a big league hitter – a car for those who'd find a Mercedes 500SL altogether too polite and pampering. It may have put on a little weight (about 60kg) but its 32-valve V8 engine is stronger than ever.

The extra muscle is largely a result of a longer stroke and another 440cc, while still smoother running is promised by having eight crankshaft balancer weights instead of six. Further honing includes more sound deadening and a gearbox re-engineered for an easier shift.

Outputs, unsurprisingly, are at an all-time high for a 928, respectively 20bhp and 45lb ft of torque up on the GT's. The GTS's 350bhp, however, is developed 500rpm lower at 5700rpm and its 362lb ft of torque 150rpm higher at 4250rpm.

The top speed round Millbrook's speed bowl of 168mph is 4mph better than the GT posted – but achieved with a similar measure of granite stability – and virtually matches the factory's 170mph flat road claim. In our hands, only two cars have gone faster at the Bedfordshire proving ground and both were Ferrari Testarossas, the latest 512TR clocking an astonishing 175mph. That said, it does cost twice as much as the Porsche.

Maranello's fastest also eclipses the GTS in a straight sprint from rest, storming to 60

and 100mph in 5.0 and 10.7secs respectively against the 928's relatively relaxed 5.4 and 14.3secs. As you'd hope, the GTS beats its predecessor to the punch by a couple of tenths to 60mph but, disappointingly, is almost a second down at 100mph, the GT recording a storming 13.4secs. Despite holding a 1mph advantage in top speed, there's no danger of the GTS usurping the 911 Turbo (4.7/11.4secs) as Porsche's peak performer.

If you want evidence that standing start figures are a poor guide to real-world performance, though, the GTS is happy to provide it. You only have to look at the fourth-gear 50–70mph time of 3.7secs to understand the magnitude of its overtaking ability. Even the Ferrari has to drop down to third to match it (3.7secs); in fourth it's left trailing with a time of 5.5secs. This is no trick of the torque curve but it does point to the fact that the Porsche has snappier gearing than the Testarossa. Take 80–100mph in fifth – the Porsche does it in 5.9secs, the 512TR takes 7.5secs.

It's the deep-chested dig of the 32-valve V8 that makes the biggest impression on the road. With small throttle openings, the unit feels curiously torpid and apathetic but, in league with the clean response and taut driveline, this makes driving in traffic less of a bind than with some rivals. Push it towards the floor with anything approaching deliberation and its immense reserves are marshalled progressively into spine-tingling service. Far from there being any troughs in the delivery, usable power seems to be flowing over the sides. All out, there's little question that the GTS possesses Porsche's most vigorous ever V8, although it's far from the smoothest or most musical. The howling, burbling voice is there all right but is submerged beneath a hash of ancillary transmission noise, which, while never all that loud, is more industrial than inspirational.

As already intimated, the GTS is geared for performance rather than parsimony and,

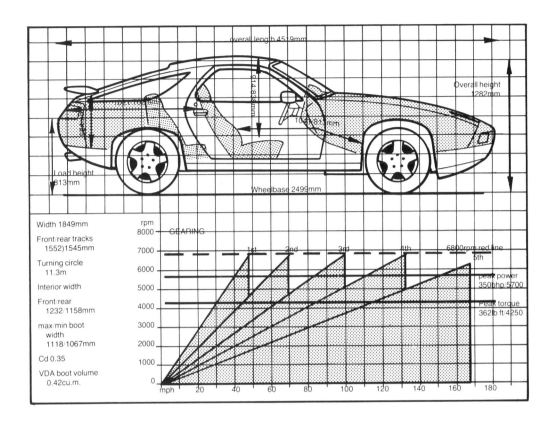

Dimensions of the 928.

given the extent of the former, few will be shocked by its 14.8mpg overall. But impressive as the Porsche's thirst is, it's no more profligate than the Ferrari's 14.7mpg or indeed, the 938 GT's 14.2mpg. Our best return of 19.9mpg shows that there is some scope for improvement, but not much. Even with an 86-litre (18.9-gallon) tank, the practical range is about 370 miles.

The 928's five-speed gearchange isn't all that heavy but, despite Porsche's best efforts to refine it, remains clonky and prone to baulking if the driver isn't neat and positive. More taxing in its long-windedness than its weight, the clutch has a reasonably progressive, if late, take-up and plenty of bite during fast shifts.

More than with previous 928s, the GTS's chassis places far greater emphasis on grip and stability than balance and adjustability. Which isn't to say that one of the great-handling supercars has been tainted by shopping car sensibilities but, with still wider tyres and an effective electronically controlled limited slip differential (PDS), wild power slides are much harder to provoke than they once were. The system isn't so protective that it kills all the fun, though. You can zip out of junctions with little drama but if you're determined to go sideways you will; few big cars feel better on opposite lock than a 928.

As power assistance goes, the Porsche's is about as unintrusive as it comes and leaves feedback well resolved and largely unsullied. Helm responses feel precise and meaty, too.

SPECIFICATION

ENGINE
Layout	8 cyls in vee, 5397cc
Max power	350bhp/5700rpm
Max torque	362lb ft/4250rpm
Specific output	65bhp/litre
Power to weight	216bhp/tonne
Installation	longitudinal, front, rear-wheel drive
Made of	alloy head and block
Bore/stroke	100/85.9mm
Comp ratio	10.4:1
Valves	4 per cyl, dohc
Ignition and fuel	LH-Jetronic, catalyst

GEARBOX
Type	5-speed manual
Ratios/mph per 1000rpm	
1st	3.77/7.0
2nd	2.52/10.5
3rd	1.79/14.8
4th	1.36/19.5
5th	1.00/26.5
Final drive	2.73:1

SUSPENSION
Front	double wishbones, coil springs, gas-filled dampers, anti-roll bar
Rear	upper transverse links, lower semi-trailing arms, Weissach axle, gas-filled dampers, anti-roll bar

STEERING
Type	rack and pinion, progressive power assistance
Lock to lock	3.0 turns

BRAKES
Front	322mm ventilated discs
Rear	299mm ventilated discs
Anti-lock	std

WHEELS AND TYRES
Size	
Front	7.5J × 17
Rear	9J × 17ins
Made of	forged alloy
Tyres	front 225/45 ZR17 rear 255/40 ZR17
Spare	space saver

WEIGHT
Kerb (incl half tank)	1600kg
Distribution f/r	52/48%
Max. payload	n/a
Max towing weight	1600kg

MADE AND SOLD BY
Dr Ing hcF Porsche AG, 7000 Porschestrasse 42, Stuttgart-Zuffenhausen, West Germany. Available in UK through Porsche Cars GB Ltd, Bath Road, Calcot, Reading, Berkshire, RG3 7SE. Tel: 0734 303666

PERFORMANCE

The figures were taken at the Lotus proving ground, Millbrook, with the odometer reading 15,200 miles. Autocar & Motor test results are protected by world copyright and may not be reproduced without the editor's written permission.

MAXIMUM SPEEDS
Top gear	168mph/6340rpm
4th	133/6800
3rd	100/6800
2nd	71/6800
1st	48/6800

ACCELERATION FROM REST
True mph	Secs	Speedo mph
30	2.2	32
40	2.9	42
50	4.1	52
60	5.4	62
70	7.1	73
80	8.9	83
90	11.2	90
100	14.3	103
110	17.5	113
120	21.5	123
130	27.7	133
Standing qtr mile	14.1 secs/100mph	
Standing km	25.7 secs/127mph	
30–70mph through gears	4.9 secs	

ACCELERATION IN EACH GEAR
mph	top	4th	3rd	2nd
10–30	–	4.6	3.3	2.3
20–40	6.0	4.2	3.1	2.1
30–50	5.8	4.1	2.8	2.0
40–60	5.8	3.9	2.7	2.0
50–70	5.9	3.7	2.7	2.6
60–80	5.8	3.9	2.8	–
70–90	5.7	4.0	3.2	–
80–100	5.9	4.2	–	–
90–110	6.4	4.6	–	–
100–120	6.8	5.4	–	–
110–130	7.6	7.1	–	–
120–140	9.3	–	–	–
130–150	11.5	–	–	–

BRAKES
Distance travelled under max braking (track surface: dry)

	Anti-lock	yes
30mph	8.8m	
50mph	25.0m	
70mph	48.9m	
st qtr mile (98mph)	102.7m	

FADE TESTS
Consecutive brake applications at 0.5g retardation from st qtr terminal speed

(figures on the right represent pedal pressures)

	40lb
	20lb
	10lb
	0lb

FUEL CONSUMPTION
Overall mpg on test	14.8
Best/worst on test	19.9/8.2
Touring	19.9
Range	376 miles
Govt test (mpg):	
urban	13.6
56mph	28.7
75mph	23.5
Tank capacity	52 litres (18.9 galls)

WHAT IT COSTS

PRICES
List price	£64,998
Total as tested	£64,998

EQUIPMENT
(prices in **bold type** denote option fitted to test car)

Electric sunroof	★
Adjustable seatbelt height	★
Seatbelt pre-tensioners	★
Electrically adjustable mirrors	★
Auto-reverse radio/cassette player	★
Electric aerial	★
10 speakers	★
Alloy wheels	★
Adjustable steering column	★
Electric windows all round	★
One-shot driver's window	★
Central locking on any door	★
Height and tilt adj driver's seat	★
Driver's seat lumbar adjustment	–
Electric seat adjustment	★
Anti-theft system	★
Anti-lock brakes	★
Cruise control	★
Leather trim	★
Traction control	★
Trip computer	★
Heater seats	£291.95
Air conditioning	★

★ standard   – not available

WARRANTY
24 months unlimited mileage, 10 years anti-corrosion

SERVICING
Major service time	12,000 miles, 5.9 hrs

PARTS COSTS
Oil filter	£13.41
Air filter	£31.04
Set of spark plugs	£44.78
Brake pads (front)	£136.02
Brake pads/shoes (rear)	£108.05/38.33
Exhaust (excluding catalyst)	£1215.42
Door mirror glass	£48.12
Windscreen	£422.13
Headlamp unit	178.46
Front wing	£648.66
Rear bumper	£800.28

Belying its size and weight, the GTS is an easy car to place accurately in a bend and one that appears to have inexhaustible composure: it turns in with crisp fluency and has terrific body control. A mild tendency for the front wheels to run down cambers needs watching down narrow, twisty lanes but grip, even in the wet, is extraordinary. As, in many respects, is the ride which, although very firm, never feels harsh or jittery.

Braking, as you might reasonably expect with massive ventilated discs all round, is vastly powerful but the spongy pedal feel saps confidence – initially at least.

Jaguar-style refinement has never been on the 928's agenda and neither is it with the GTS. Even on a light throttle the engine can be heard, but this is more a reflection of the reduction in road roar than any increase in mechanical noise.

Cosmetically plusher and better equipped for the GTS, the 928's cabin design has changed hardly at all over the years. What started out as peerless switchgear ergonomics seems a tad clumsy now, but for instrumentation presentation and clarity, driving position and seat comfort, the Porsche is the paragon it always was. Visibility is good, too, and the feeling of solidity the cabin exudes is nothing short of remarkable. The fit of the carpet on the broad sills looks like it belongs to a cheaper car, though.

Only the sadistic would call the 928 a four-seater, but the rear accommodation is fine in an emergency or for small children and, in its intended role as a mile-eating express, space for two people and their luggage is ample.

The equipment list is as thorough as a £65,000 price tag would signify and includes air conditioning, cruise control, leather upholstery, part-powered seat adjustment and an impressive-looking but ordinary-sounding 10-speaker stereo.

It would be easy to get the wrong idea about the GTS. True, it's less noisy than the

GT it supplements and totes a more comfortable ride. It's a little plusher and a little plumper. But it hasn't lost sight of what the 928 is all about and that's driving. From beneath the gloss, an even clearer focus and more uncompromising nature emerges. There might be more cosseting coupes and faster supercars but none can touch the 928 for a potent combination of driver appeal and practicality.

CREATURE COMFORTS

But if this cast a question mark over the Porsche's credentials as a long-distance cruiser, the spaciousness and habitability of the cabin went a long way towards making up for the shortfall. Considered purely as a two-seater, the 928 was magnificently roomy with massive available legroom and good headroom though the latter was in part achieved by having a very low seating position. And with the occasional rear seats folded forward, it was possible to squeeze a surprising amount of luggage behind the glass tailgate without obscuring visibility. With the rear seats in place, however, life in the back for a human cargo was somewhat cramped, especially with regard to headroom. Also, the boot shrunk to a paltry 5 cu ft or so – sufficient only for a couple of squashy bags.

When it came right down to it, though, the maximum satisfaction the 928 had to offer was aimed at one person. Once ensconced behind the leather-rimmed, three-spoke steering wheel, the driver was extremely well looked after. Cabin ergonomics hit a new high with Porsche's idea that when you adjusted the rake of the steering wheel, the whole steering column and instrument binnacle should move with it, thus maintaining a constant relationship between wheel, switchgear and instruments.

The dials and gauges contained within the

broad binnacle behind a single pane of glass, angled to eliminate stray reflections, were themselves models of presentational elegance and clarity and comprised a large speedometer and rev counter in the centre, flanked to the left by gauges for water temperature and fuel level and, to the right, oil pressure and battery charge. In short, the 928's instrumentation and control layout were as perfect as the 911's were flawed.

Another new experience for ex-911 owners was a heating and ventilation system that worked. In stark contrast to the rear-engined car's scattered profusion of sliders, the 928's controls were child's play with a rotary knob for the five-speed fan and upper and lower sliders governing temperature and distribution respectively. Vents were located in every conceivable position – not just in the footwells and beneath the windscreen but in the door armrests. These could be individually opened or closed and directed either towards your face or at the side windows for demisting. The system was not perfect – temperature regulation went from hot to cold too abruptly and the booster fan was noisy – but by 911 standards, it was a revelation.

As was the level of standard equipment. You did not have to fork out for air conditioning (which even kept things cool in the glovebox), a stereo radio/cassette, cruise control, electric windows and door mirrors, alloy wheels or power-assisted steering. Other thoughtful touches included the illuminated vanity mirror, a tiny torch built into the ignition key and door armrests that could be extended for extra comfort, simultaneously permitting access to a hidden cubby below.

All in all, the 928 racked up close to full marks for cabin design, but decor was another matter. Undeniably different and arresting, the loud pop-art check pattern of the seats' cloth inserts was horribly overpowering in practice and almost

The early 928's rear seats weren't the last word in subtlety.

laughably incongruous. Unless you actually liked the idea of being able to play chess on the seat cushions, plain leather was an essential option and, in recognition of the check seats' unpopularity, soon became standard. Aesthetic predilections aside, the 928 was beautifully built and finished, from the immaculate fit of the curvy body panels to the flawless finish of the paintwork to the artful blending of leather and plastic trim panels and the high quality feel of the switchgear.

928S

The 928 truly hard-driving enthusiasts wanted to get to grips with was not made until 1980. Granted the S suffix, in time-honoured Zuffenhausen tradition, this version

'The 928 S' has appeared on Porsche
GB press cars since the very first
928 S.

The 928's trademark was its 'shark's-
eye' flip-up headlights. Auxiliary
driving lights are integrated with the
indicators.

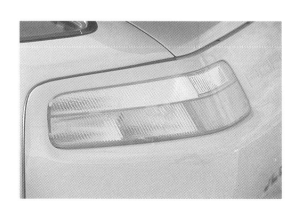

The new-style tail lights gave the 928
a fresh lease of life.

928S (1980)

Engine
Longitudinal, front, rear-wheel drive

Capacity	4,664cc, 8-cyl in vee
Bore/Stroke	97/79mm
Compression ratio	10.0:1
Head/Block	Al alloy/Al alloy
Valve gear	Sohc, 2 valves per cylinder
Fuel and Ignition	Electronic ignition, Bosch K-Jetronic fuel injection
Max Power	300bhp at 5,500rpm
Max Torque	283lb ft at 4,500rpm

Gearbox
Five-speed manual

Suspension
Front	Independent, double wishbones, telescopic dampers with co-axial coil springs, anti-roll bar
Rear	Independent, lower wishbones, upper transverse link (Porsche–Weissach patent geometry), coil springs, telescopic dampers, anti-roll bar

Steering
Rack and pinion, power assistance

Brakes
Front	Ventilated discs
Rear	Ventilated discs
ABS	No

Wheels and Tyres
Cast alloy, 7.0×16in Pirelli P7 225/50 VR16

Dimensions
Length	175in (4,445mm)
Width	72.3in (1,836mm)
Height	51.8in (1,316mm)
Weight	3,615lb (1,640kg)

had a larger capacity (4.7-litre) engine, more power, visual changes and a more comprehensive specification. Visually, the modifications were subtle but significant, the 928S acquiring a front air dam with two small rectangular slots for brake cooling and a rear lip spoiler made of polyurethane and claimed to give a lower drag coefficient of 0.38. Also new were the flat disc style 16in alloy wheels shod with the 225/50 section

The 928S Series 2 for 1984 – more power and equipment.

P7s of the original car (which, in turn, had its rubber down-graded to 215/60 P6s) and discreet side rubbing strips to protect the alloy doors and front wings.

Also low-key but pertinent to the evolution of the model were the alterations to the interior. These included the adoption of a thermostatically controlled heating and air conditioning system, a new four-spoke steering wheel and the standardization of electrically powered seats with height, reach and backrest adjustment.

Not so subtle were the changes under the bonnet where the all-alloy, water-cooled V8 went from 4,474cc to 4,664cc (achieved by stretching the bore of the linerless cylinders from 95 to 97mm) and, in line with all 1980 928s, the compression ratio was raised from 8.5:1 to 10.0:1, requiring the use of 4-star instead of 2-star petrol. Exclusive to the S, however, were re-profiled camshafts and,

along with the other changes, these raised the power output by 25 per cent to 300bhp at 5,900rpm and peak torque by 10 per cent to 283.4lb ft at 4,500rpm. Bosch K-Jetronic injection was retained.

The S certainly gave the 928 what it most needed – more performance. Enough, in fact, to yank the Porsche from last to first in the GT premier league. A top speed of 155mph (249km/h), 0–60mph (0–96km/h) in 6.2secs, 0–100mph (0–160km/h) in 14.8secs and 50–70mph (80–113km/h) in top in 7.3secs and gave the opposition a fright and the driver the biggest Porsche-derived thrill he could experience this side of a 911 Turbo.

The extra power showed just how good the chassis was, too. I wrote *Motor*'s 1980 test of the 928 and can do no better than to recount the road test team's views about the handling:

While, in normal driving on dry roads,

49

the handling is biased towards mild understeer, the determined driver can use the extra power of the S to balance the car's attitude through a fast bend and, if conditions permit, power past the apex on a few degrees of easily-held opposite lock. Mid-corner stability and poise are excellent, too, the Porsche–Weissach rear toe in axle geometry ensuring that there is no instant over-steer should you lift-off the throttle: nor do bumps exert even the slightest influence over the driver's chosen line. In the wet, the P7s retain enough of their grip for the 928S to be driven quickly and safely though, obviously, with so much power on tap, a delicate touch is required, and if tail slides are provoked, it isn't wise to let them get too pronounced.

In 1984, the 928S2 arrived toting optional ABS anti-lock brakes, the latest Bosch LH-Jetronic fuel injection with overrun cut-off and 310bhp at 5,900rpm supported by 295lb ft of torque at 4,100rpm. Top speed went up to 158mph (254km/h) and the 0–60mph (0–96km/h) time down to just under six and a half seconds.

ROAD TEST
Reproduced from *Motor*
Road Tests Annual 1985

PORSCHE 928 SERIES 2

Conceived as a some-day replacement for the aged 911 but set in the mould of a heavy-weight Grand Touring car, Porsche's 928 has always been a paradox. Unable to match the raw driving charisma of its in-house rival and outclassed in the refinement stakes by Jaguar and Mercedes, it fell between two

stools – a touch too soft in character to wean 911 die-hards away from their anachronistic driving machine, a shade too noisy and bumpy to poach sales from the ranks of luxury supercoupés. In its UK debut year it became 1978 Car of the Year, but potential buyers were less convinced.

Of course Porsche didn't leave it at that. For 1980 they unleashed the bespoilered 928S, with slightly greater engine capacity, 25 per cent more power, and an uprated chassis to match. This demolished complaints about the original car's performance and satisfied those who'd expected the 928 to be a no-holds-barred roadburner from the start. At the same time the ordinary 928's identity was nudged further in the other direction. Engine revisions boosted torque and economy with-out affecting maximum power, while chassis alterations included a reversion to narrower 60-series tyres in place of the previous knob-bly and rumbly 50-series P7s – these remain-ing as standard, however, on the more overtly aggressive 928S.

It now seemed that Porsche had themselves covered both ways. By 1982, however, market preference for the more powerful model had become such that in the summer of that year the 'soft option' was quietly phased out. The 'S' version became the standard, and only, model.

Enter the 928S series 2, a designation that is unique to the UK market by virtue of its anti-lock braking, an extra-cost option else-where but supplied as standard over here. Other '84 model-year changes are common to all markets, notably small increases in power and torque, combined with the inevitable economy gains, and a new (optional) auto-matic transmission with four ratios to replace the previous three-speed. Minor enhancements to trim and equipment levels complete the picture for UK customers.

In outline specification the 1984 model 928S – series 2 or otherwise – remains essen-tially unaltered. The 4,664cc all-alloy V8 engine is mounted up front and drives to the rear wheels through a twin-plate clutch, a torque-tube enclosed propshaft and a trans-axle at the rear – five speed manual, or, as in our test car, four-speed automatic. Large ventilated disc brakes at each corner are fed by a front/rear split circuit and prevented from lock-up by Bosch's latest Anti-locking System (ABS). The rack and pinion steering is power-assisted as standard. Front suspension is by double wishbones and coils, while at the rear there is an upper transverse link and a lower wishbone on each side, with the additional refinement of Porsche-Weissach patented geometry. This is designed to cause the loaded rear wheel to toe-in, not toe-out as is normal, when slowing suddenly in mid-corner, thus preventing sudden oversteer. Coil springs are also used at the rear, and there's an anti-roll bar at each end.

Priced at £30,679 whichever transmission you choose (despite the 928S's macho temperament, UK buyers apparently prefer the auto to the manual by more than three to one) the 928S occupies a price sector where automatic rivals are somewhat scarce – really only the Mercedes 500SEC (£31,890) and the De Tomaso Longchamp (£29,058). You could save yourself quite a packet by opting for the BMW 635CSiA (£23,995) or the keenly-priced Jaguar XJ-S HE (£21,752), but failing that you'd have to pay out more for an Aston Martin V8 (£42,498), Bristol Brigand (£49,827) or Ferrari 400i (£43,561): Maranello's Mondial 2+2 is a more natural rival at £29,732, but is only available with manual transmission.

Alterations to the sohc per bank V8 are confined to the adoption of Bosch's latest fuel

The 928 was entrusted with the job of killing off the 911. It didn't succeed.

injection system, the LH-Jetronic with over-run fuel cut-off, and a new ETZ ignition system, but the improved combustion that they provide lifts maximum power from 300 bhp at 5,900 rpm to 310 bhp at the same engine speed while torque climbs from 283 lb ft at 4,500 rpm to 295 lb ft at 4,100 rpm.

In the case of the manual transmission car we don't doubt Porsche's claim of a 3 mph increase in maximum speed (to 158.5 mph). But for once we were sceptical of Porsche's claim for a similar increase on the auto, bearing in mind that whereas the old three-speed was almost perfectly geared for its claimed maximum (152 mph, corresponding closely to peak power revs), the 4-speed's much longer top gear stride would leave it a full 800 rpm short of the 5,900 rpm power peak. Our doubts were confirmed at the Millbrook test track where the 928's best lap speed was no better than 149.1 mph, too great a deficit on the claimed 155 mph to be explained solely by the effects of cornering forces round Millbrook's two mile circle. Since the weather conditions were not unfavourable and the Concessionaires have been unable to find any fault on the car, we can only assume that on this one occasion the factory's claim err on the optimistic side.

Even so, 149.1 mph is bettered only by the Jaguar's 152.4 mph among our chosen rivals, even those with manual gearboxes failing to match the Porsche. And on acceleration the series 2 takes full advantage of its better spread of ratios. Mash the throttle to the floor and the 928 wheelspins off the line to reach 30 mph in just 2.7 sec, 60 in 6.5 and 100mph in 16.3 sec. Try your damnedest in the manual Ferrari Mondial and you'd just about stay with it, likewise perhaps the latest auto version of the Aston Martin (our figures date back to 1978). Nothing else we've tested would get much of a look in: once rolling the Jaguar would be the Porsche's shadow all the way up the speed range and eventually

overtake it, but it can't match the German car's smart step-off from rest. And only the Porsche delivers it ultimate performance with the gear lever left in D. True, the auto change-up from first to second occurs at barely 5,000 rpm but there's not much you can do about that anyway, since the 'box doesn't provide a first gear hold facility; and with the other two intermediates held to only a whisker short of the 6,000 rpm red line, there's nothing to be gained by delaying the shifts manually.

For squirting past traffic queues on country roads, full-throttle kickdown is devastatingly effective – the product of snap responses and a readiness to change down into the lowest possible gear even at already high road speeds. Full-throttle downchanges to second, for example, are available at up to 66 mph. No rival can beat the 928's 2.2 sec 30–50 mph time. On an autobahn you can be ambling along at 110 mph with the tachometer showing a lazy 3,600 rpm: stamp the throttle and the instant downshift to third will have you up to 120 mph in little more than four seconds . . .

Drive it thus, and the 928S is no paragon of refinement. We liked the sound the engine made when driven in anger, but it leaves you in no doubt of its aggressively sporting nature. Even at tickover there's a delectable, meaty rumble from the exhaust to remind you of the latent power. Use that power to the full and the radio will be drowned by the fierce, loud bellow from under the bonnet – not harsh or rough, but a world apart from the distant hum of a Jaguar, Mercedes or BMW.

Most that's been said so far concerns the 928's performance on full throttle. Drive it moderately, however, and it shows another side to its character. Easy-starting and untemperamental, the docility of its responses can even extend to an impression of laziness. There is more torque converter slip than is usual, which means that at pottering speeds a modest prod of the throttle merely lifts the revs without much increasing your speed over the ground. It takes a longer shove of the pedal than you'd expect, to trigger a part-throttle downchange. So in give-and-take use the Mercedes-based transmission isn't as vividly responsive as, say, the ZF four-speed used in current BMWs. With this one, if you want it to operate in performance mode you've got to send it a strong signal with your right foot. Otherwise it'll stay in economy mode, shifting up early, staying in a high gear. There were few complaints about gearchange quality, however, and neither was there any particular pattern to the odd occasions when shifts were less than ideally smooth. Smooth and pleasant to handle, the T-bar gear selector permits unobstructed down-changes from D to third; but it fails to protect against inadvertent selection of Neutral when changing up.

Performance apart, the automatic version of the series 2 promises a useful gain in economy, stemming primarily from the top gear stride that's lifted from the 26.5 to 30.5 mph per 1,000 rpm, as well as the engine alterations. Our hard-driven test car couldn't quite manage Porsche's claimed 12 per cent improvement, but the eight per cent we did get – from 15.8 to 17.1 mpg – is not to be sneezed at. That's better than the less accelerative Jaguar's 16.3 mpg and not far off the 17.5 mpg we recorded with the Mercedes 500SEC, though we'd expect that even in its automatic form the BMW 635CSi (22.5 mpg as a manual) would put them all to shame. Driven steadily on longer runs we'd expect the Porsche's touring consumption to better 20 mpg, permitting a range approaching 400 miles on each 18.9 gallon filling of four-star.

One thing that needed no improvement for '84 was the 928's handling. Its combination of swift, sharp steering, fine chassis poise and the staunch grip of 225/50 VR16 Pirelli P7s on each corner makes it simultaneously one of the most forgiving and most rewarding of the current supercar crop. Power assisted for easy parking yet meatily weighted on the move, the steering feels reassuring right from the start (even if, in common with most assisted systems, it doesn't produce much in the way of genuine feel in extremis, such as when the front wheels start to lose grip on a slippery patch). The chassis, however, is never likely to betray you. High though they are, it's a supercar whose limits you feel you can explore without fear. As you start to do so, there's a gentle build-up of understeer – stronger in tight curves – and you can always lift off the throttle to tighten your line without fear of upsetting the car's balance: not once did we experience unwanted lift-off oversteer. Yet if you've a mind to, through tight bends you can power the tail out into progressive and marvellously controllable oversteering slides. On a clean wet road these characteristics remain much the same at an only moderately reduced level of grip, and here the gentle initial throttle action and not-too-sensitive kickdown help avoid any unplanned drama when accelerating on the turn. Only on a really greasy kind of wetness does the 928 feel edgy, unsure which end to let go first, though even then there's ample seat of the pants feel to telegraph its intentions.

It's then, too, that you'll most appreciate the ABS. Unfortunately we were unable to carry out our braking distance tests in the time available, but on a dry surface the 928 stops so well anyway that it takes a very deliberate effort to bring the anti-lock system into play at all. When you succeed, you notice that the pedal modulation operates at a far higher frequency than other systems we've tried. Unfortunately, though, it shares with them the usual rather soft pedal action, though its progression is unimpaired.

Not much else about the 928S has changed from the auto that featured in our Group Test of August last year. It remains a strongly constructed 2+2 that provides acres of space for two people and their luggage or can, at a pinch, carry four compliant and not too large

Seats adjustable for height, reach and recline, together with a height-adjustable wheel, allow all drivers to achieve an ideal posture.

adults over short distances, with ample storage space for oddments, most of it lidded or lockable. New for '84 is a remote release button for the rear tailgate.

Ride quality remains uncompromisingly firm, in keeping with the sporting side of its character but, especially around town, too hard for comfort for what also purports to be a luxury coupé. Damping control at speed is superb but even then the car moves with bumps rather than absorbing them. Shapely seats that are electrically adjustable for height, reach and recline, together with a height adjustable wheel, permit all shapes of driver to tailor an ideal posture at the wheel, though one tester found that longer journeys showed up the need for a little more lumbar support. Because the height adjuster only

raises the rear of the seat (at some cost in under-thigh support) even our shorter testers tended to leave it on its lower setting, but this does aggravate the difficulty of positioning the car's bulbous shape when parking or when driving along narrow lanes. Thickish pillars all round can occasionally be a disadvantage and the headlights are weak on dip, but by supercar standards seeing out is not generally a problem.

Certainly there's never any difficulty in reading the impeccable instrument display. This is housed in a binnacle that moves with the wheel when it's adjusted for height, along with the important minor switchgear, which thus always remains within fingertip reach of the wheel.

As ever we remain relatively unimpressed

PERFORMANCE

WEATHER CONDITIONS

Wind	8–13mph
Temperature	52°F 11°C
Barometer	29.5 in Hg 999 mbar
Surface	Dry tarmacadam

MAXIMUM SPEEDS

	mph	kph
Banked circuit	149.1	239.9
Best ¼ mile	150.4	242.0
Terminal Speeds:		
at ¼ mile	96	154
at kilometre	125	201
Speed in gears (at 6,000rpm)		
1st	41*	66
2nd	76	122
3rd	128	206

*at 5,000rpm

ACCELERATION FROM REST

mph	sec	kph	sec
0–30	2.7	0–40	2.2
0–40	3.7	0–60	3.5
0–50	4.9	0–80	4.9
0–60	6.5	0–100	6.9
0–70	8.2	0–120	9.0
0–80	10.2	0–140	12.1
0–90	13.0	0–160	16.2
0–100	16.3	0–180	20.8
0–110	20.0		
0–120	24.2		
Standing ¼	14.9	Standing km	26.8

ACCELERATION IN KICKDOWN

mph	sec	kph	sec
20–40	2.1	40–60	1.3
30–50	2.2	60–80	1.4
40–60	2.8	80–100	2.0
50–70	3.3	100–120	2.1
60–80	3.7	120–140	3.1
70–90	4.8	140–160	4.1
80–100	6.1	160–180	4.6
90–100	7.0		
100–120	7.9		

FUEL CONSUMPTION

Overall	17.1mpg
	16.5 litres 100km
Govt tests	16.9mpg (urban)
	32.8mpg (56mph)
	27.0mpg (75mph)
Fuel grade	98 octane
	4 star rating
Tank capacity	18.9 galls
	86 litres
Max range*	397 miles
	639km
Test distance	1,236 miles
	1,989km

*Based on estimated 21mpg touring consumption

NOISE

	dBA	Motor rating*
30mph	67	13
50mph	72	18
70mph	75	23
Maximum‡	88	56

*A rating where 1=30 dBA, and 100=96 dBA, and where double the number means double the loudness
‡Peak noise level under full-throttle acceleration in 2nd

SPEEDOMETER (mph)

Speedo	30	40	50	60	70	80	90	100
True mph	29	39	49	59	69	79	90	100

WEIGHT

	cwt	kg
Unladen weight*	30.3	1,540
Weight as tested	34.0	1,728

*with fuel for approx 50 miles

Performance tests carried out by *Motor's* staff at the Motor Industry Research Association proving ground, Lindley, and at Vauxhall Proving Ground, Millbrook.

Test Data: World Copyright reserved. No reproduction in whole or part without written permission.

GENERAL SPECIFICATION

ENGINE

Cylinders	V8
Capacity	4,664cc (284.4 cu in)
Bore/stroke	97/78.9mm
	(3.82/3.11in)
Cooling	Water
Block	Aluminium alloy
Head	Aluminium alloy
Valves	Sohc per bank
Cam drive	Toothed belt
Compression	10.4:1
Fuel system	Bosch LH-Jetronic injection
Ignition	Electronic
Bearings	5 main
Max power	310bhp (DIN) at 5,900rpm
Max torque	295lb ft (DIN) at 4,100rpm

TRANSMISSION

Type	4-speed automatic
Internal ratios and mph/1000rpm	
Top	1.000:1/30.5
3rd	1.436:1/21.3
2nd	2.412:1/12.7
1st	3.676:1/8.3
Rev	5.139:1
Final drive	2.357:1

BODY/CHASSIS

Construction	Steel monocoque with alloy doors, bonnet and front wings
Protection	7-year Long-Life guarantee

SUSPENSION

Front	Independent by double wishbones: strut dampers with co-axial coil springs: anti-roll bar
Rear	Independent by lower wishbones, upper transverse links and Porsche-Weissach patent geometry: coil springs: anti-roll bar

STEERING

Type	Rack and pinion
Assistance	Yes

BRAKES

Front	Ventilated discs, 11.1in dia
Rear	Ventilated discs, 11.4in dia
Park	On rear, separate drums
Servo	Yes
Circuit	Split front/rear
Rear valve	ABS anti-lock system
Adjustment	Automatic

WHEELS/TYRES

Type	Alloy, 7 × 16in
Tyres	Pirelli P7, 225/50 VR16
Pressures	36/44 psi F/R

ELECTRICAL

Battery	12V, 88 Ah
Earth	Negative
Generator	Alternator, 90A
Fuses	36
Headlights	
type	Halogen retractable
dip	110W total
main	120W total

Make: Porsche. **Model:** 928S series 2 auto
Makers: Dr Ing h c F. Porsche AG, 7000 Stuttgart-Zuffenhausen, Porschestrasse 42, West Germany
UK Importers: Porsche Cars GB Ltd, Richfield Ave, Reading, Berks RG1 8PH. Tel: 0734-595411
Price: £24,625.00 plus £2,052.08 car tax plus £4,001.56 VAT equals £30,678.64

with the standard air conditioning, which may do a fine job of refrigeration in Summer but can't provide the bi-level temperature split you need during the remainder of the year: in this instance, even to maintain a steady overall warmth seemed beyond the capabilities of our (possibly faulty) test car. Build quality generally, however, was up to Porsche's usual high standards with tastefully chosen materials, superb detailing, and a fine balance between luxury and function. Luxury is certainly the keynote of the appointments list, which includes electric operation for the seats, door mirrors, windows and door locks; air conditioning; cruise control; a high-tech Blaupunkt stereo radio/cassette player; headlamp washers; and adjustable steering.

It's on the road that the balance tilts firmly in favour of function. The price of the 928's terrific roadability is a suspension that not only feels uncompromisingly firm as we've already discussed, but sounds it too. The tyres thump over sharp-edged disturbances, rumble and roar over all but the most finely textured surfaces. Of other potential sources of intrusion, wind noise is negligible while the engine, splendidly vocal under hard acceleration, is well muted when cruising.

For our money we wouldn't have a Porsche 928S automatic. We'd have the manual instead. As a manual, the 928 has resolved its one-time identity crisis to become a superbly rewarding driver's supercar – and one which, by those lights, is more civilised and practical than most alternatives.

Automatic transmission merely clouds the issue again. Don't misunderstand us. The Porsche's Mercedes-derived 'box is a fine unit if an auto is what you really want. But the automatic option implies an altogether more relaxed style of motoring. It also sets the Porsche on a collision course with Jaguar, BMW and Mercedes. None of these could stay with the Porsche on a foot-to-the-floor cross country blast, but they all offer a quieter,

smoother ride around town and on the motorway. In the 928S as a luxury grand tourer, the automatic soft option mixes uneasily with its aggressive engine and intrusive suspension. In the 928S as a supercar driving machine – and that means as a manual – they wouldn't matter a damn.

The paradox continues.

928S4

Far more telling, however, was the introduction of the S4 in 1987, some ten years after the original model's Geneva Show debut. Just when it seemed as if the competition was catching up, the 928 eased into a higher gear. It looked better and went faster, boasting a 5-litre engine with four valves per cylinder driven by twin overhead camshafts atop each bank of cylinders.

There were other mechanical changes. The cylinder heads had slightly shallower combustion chambers, larger intake and exhaust valves, a narrower angle between the valves and revised valve timing. Power went up a further 10bhp to 320bhp and torque an additional 22lb ft to 37lb ft. Top speed, however, shot up by a seemingly disproportionate amount from 158 to 165mph (265km/h) and the time it took to sprint from rest to 60mph fell to around the six second mark. But then the changes to the bodywork were more than merely cosmetic. They cut drag by 13 per cent.

The sheet metal remained as before but the plastic nose section was re-contoured to incorporate auxiliary light clusters that were more nearly flush and a smoother bottom section without the previous lip spoiler. This gave more effective airflow management, guiding air under the car and over the new, smooth belly pain instead of forcing it to the sides. Likewise, the new plastic tail section was smoother and rounder with larger and near-flush tail light clusters and

The 928S took the regular car's already exciting performance on to a higher level. But there was a lot more to come.

	BMW 850i	Jaguar XJR–S	Porsche 928S4
Top speed (mph/km/h)	157/253	157/253	159/256
Acceleration from rest, secs			
0–30 (0–48)	2.9	2.9	2.7
0–40 (0–64)	4.1	4.1	3.7
0–50 (0–80)	5.3	5.5	4.9
0–60 (0–96)	7.2	7.0	6.4
0–70 (0–113)	9.0	8.9	8.1
0–80 (0–129)	11.0	11.0	10.6
0–90 (0–145)	13.5	13.5	13.2
0–100 (0–160)	16.7	16.4	16.1
0–110 (0–177)	20.0	20.2	19.5
0–120 (0–193)	24.8	24.7	25.5
0–130 (0–209)	29.3	30.4	—
Stg qtr mile	15.3	15.3	15.0
Stg km	27.2	27.3	27.8
30–70 (48–113)	6.1	6.0	5.4
Overall mpg (l/100km)	14.4 (19.6)	12.6 (22.5)	17.4 (16.3)

a contoured lower section to further clean up the airflow.

All this, however, seemed like the very essence of understatement next to the S4's rear wing jutting defiantly from the trailing edge of the tailgate glass which, while modest by Sierra Cosworth standards, gave the 928 a sharp visual lift. Still on the trail of aerodynamic improvement, the new 'intelligent' cooling system introduced a set of

928 S4 (1986)

Engine
Longitudinal, front, rear-wheel drive
Capacity	4,957cc, 8-cyl in vee
Bore/Stroke	100/79mm
Compression ratio	10.0:1
Head/Block	Al alloy/Al alloy
Valve gear	Dohc, 4 valves per cylinder
Fuel and Ignition	Electronic ignition, Bosch LII-Jetronic fuel injection
Max Power	320bhp at 6,000rpm
Max Torque	317lb ft at 3,000rpm

Gearbox
Five-speed manual

Suspension
Front	Independent, double wishbones, telescopic dampers with co-axial coil springs, anti-roll bar
Rear	Independent, lower wishbones, upper transverse link (Porsche–Weissach patent geometry), coil springs, telescopic dampers, anti-roll bar

Steering
Rack and pinion, power assistance

Brakes
Front	Ventilated discs
Rear	Ventilated discs
ABS	Standard

Wheels and Tyres
Cast alloy, 7.0×16in front, 8×16in rear. 225/50 VR16 front, 245/45 VR16 rear

Dimensions
Length	178in (4,519mm)
Width	72.3in (1,836mm)
Height	51.8in (1,316mm)
Weight	3,649lb (1,655kg)

928S4 versus sports car rivals Catalytic converter models	BMW M5	Porsche 928 S4	Jaguar XJS V12	Ferrari Testarossa
Displacement/layout and cylinders	3.5/R6	5.0/V8	5.3/V12	4.9/F12
Valves per cylinder	4V	4V	2V	4V
Power output kW/bhp	232/315	235/320	194/264	272/320
at engine rpm	6,900	6,000	5,250	6,000
Maximum torque Nm	360	430	377	451
at engine rpm	4,750	3,000	2,750	4,500
Output per litre kW/l	65.6	47.4	36.3	55.0
Torque per litre Nm/l	101.8	86.7	70.6	91.3
Claimed top speed mph (km/h)	155 (250)	168 (270)	145 (233)	180 (290)
Acceleration				
0–62mph (0–100km/h)	6.3	5.9	7.6	5.8
0–1000m	26.0	25.5	n.a.	24.1
Average consumption mpg (l/100km)	23.8 (11.9)	20.8 (13.6)	18.5 (15.3)	18.7 (15.1)
Unladen weight lb (kg)	3,682 (1,670)	3,484 (1,580)	3,903 (1,770)	3,318 (1,505)

adjustable horizontal louvres between the grille and the radiator to regulate the cooling airflow – supplemented now by two variable speed electric fans instead of the previous engine-driven fan. The angle of the louvres, and therefore the amount of cooling, was determined by computer according to coolant temperature, the Freon pressure in the air conditioning system and,

if an automatic gearbox was fitted, the transmission oil temperature. The computer's job was to keep the louvres closed whenever possible for the best aerodynamic efficiency: the Cd increased from 0.34 to 0.36 with them fully open.

CLUB SPORT AND SPECIAL EQUIPMENT

The 928 had come a long way in ten years, but no one seriously believed it had yet reached the end of its career. A stripped down, lightened and mildly tweaked Club Sport version aimed at well-heeled production sportscar racers was introduced in 1988 and, shortly after that, came the Special Equipment – essentially a Club Sport for

Output per litre: 928S4 versus the best		
Porsche 928S4	5.0	47.4kW/l
BMW M5	3.5	65.6kW/l
BMW M3	2.3	62.1kW/l
Ferrari Testarossa	4.9	55.0kW/l
Audi V8	3.6	51.9kW/l

those who could not bear to be without the regular S4's luxury kit. Unsurprisingly, this rather confused model was not available in Germany and had been dreamed up specially for the UK market. Porsche's customer research in the UK indicated that typical profile customers would not buy a plain CS off the peg but they would buy one with all the goodies. So Porsche GB made it easy for them.

If, as Porsche in Germany had coyly suggested, the CS developed no more power than the ordinary S4, the importer's initiative to nullify the weight saving by putting back the equipment that had achieved much of it in the first place would have gone down as one of the most pointless exercises in recent automotive history. But the factory was not being entirely honest. No doubt anxious not to pre-empt the forthcoming 928 GT, Porsche's engineers spoke vaguely of

recalibrated camshafts with greater valve lift, modified engine management and a freer breathing exhaust system. It is unlikely that the changes added up to precisely nothing. On the contrary: in league with a 3.4 per cent shorter-striding final drive, the gains in top speed, acceleration and flexibility seemed entirely consistent with more muscle. By any standards, the 928 was now a very rapid car, capable of 164mph (264km/h) and 0–60mph (0–96km/h) in a storming 5.3secs.

This was the only other 928 I tested for *Motor* and comparisons with the first were inevitable:

> The original 928S which charmed the world's motoring press at the beginning of the decade with its peerless combination of grand touring abilities is but a distant relation of the red-raw

The 1988 928 S4 SE – short-lived forerunner to the GT.

928 GT (1988)

Engine
Longitudinal, front, rear-wheel drive
Capacity	4,957cc, 8-cyl in vee
Bore/Stroke	100/79mm
Compression ratio	10.5:1
Head/Block	Al alloy/Al alloy
Valve gear	Dohc, 4 valves per cylinder
Fuel and Ignition	Electronic ignition, Bosch LH-Jetronic fuel injection
Max Power	330bhp at 6,200rpm
Max Torque	317lb ft at 4,100rpm

Gearbox
Five-speed manual

Suspension
Front	Independent, double wishbones, telescopic dampers with co-axial coil springs, anti-roll bar
Rear	Independent, lower wishbones, upper transverse link (Porsche–Weissach patent geometry), coil springs, telescopic dampers, anti-roll bar

Steering
Rack and pinion, power assistance

Brakes
Front	Ventilated discs
Rear	Ventilated discs
ABS	Standard

Wheels and Tyres
Cast alloy, 7.0×16in front, 8×16in rear. 225/50 VR16 front, 245/45 VR16 rear

Dimensions
Length	178in (4,519mm)
Width	72.3in (1,836mm)
Height	51.8in (1,316mm)
Weight	3,439lb (1,560kg)

SE. You wouldn't want to tackle 500 miles of autobahn in this car. It would be too tiring. Think of a Shelby Mustang with handling, brakes and superb build quality, however, and you're getting closer to the mark . . .

. . . There's nothing about the hollow, slightly guttural timbre of the burbling engine note at tickover to warn the unsuspecting of what lies in wait. At rest, or trickling round town, this Porsche is docility personified.

61

928 GTS (1991)

Engine
Longitudinal, front, rear-wheel drive

Capacity	5,397cc, 8-cyl in vee
Bore/Stroke	100/86mm
Compression ratio	10.4:1
Head/Block	Al alloy/Al alloy
Valve gear	Dohc, 4 valves per cylinder
Fuel and Ignition	Electronic ignition, Bosch LH-Jetronic fuel injection
Max Power	350bhp at 5,700rpm
Max Torque	362lb ft at 4,250rpm

Gearbox
Five-speed manual

Suspension

Front	Independent, double wishbones, telescopic dampers with co-axial coil springs, anti-roll bar
Rear	Independent, lower wishbones, upper transverse link (Porsche–Weissach patent geometry), coil springs, telescopic dampers, anti-roll bar

Steering
Rack and pinion, power assistance

Brakes

Front	Ventilated discs
Rear	Ventilated discs
ABS	Standard

Wheels and Tyres
Cast alloy, 7.5×17in front, 9×17in rear. 225/45 ZR17 front, 265/40 ZR17 rear

Dimensions

Length	178in (4,519mm)
Width	72.7in (1,849mm)
Height	50.5in (1,282mm)
Weight	3,527lb (1,600kg)

Progress is smooth, well damped, al-ost anti-climactic. Feed the power in gently and the SE responds in kind, wafting forwards with almost benign indifference . . .

. . . Take to the open road, though, and it's a dramatically different story. All the ease and effortlessness experienced drifting through the suburbs suddenly vanishes like a pleasant daydream. To move fast in the SE requires a mental as well as a physical change of gear. If it's your intention to feel the carpet with your right foot you'd better tense your neck muscles in preparation. If you don't, giving the SE its head means losing yours to gravity. Heavy acceleration equals g-force, it's as simple as that. The big car growls, grabs the horizon by the collar and hauls it in. In real terms, it's quicker than a 911 Turbo and, this side of a 959 or F40, you don't get much quicker than that. The ordinary S4 feels tame by comparison.

In fact, the SE was nothing so much as a dry run for the 928GT introduced at the beginning of 1990 with an 'official' 330bhp and a rationalized catalogue of SE creature comforts, including a sophisticated on-board computer called the Porsche Information and Diagnostic System which continuously monitored all the car's main systems, even giving out a warning for low tyre pressure.

The finest 928 of all was launched in the spring of 1992. The GTS had a 5.4-litre version of the quad cam, 32-valve V8 pushing out a formidable 340bhp and 368lb ft of torque, revised rear-end styling and new Carrera Turbo-style alloy wheels.

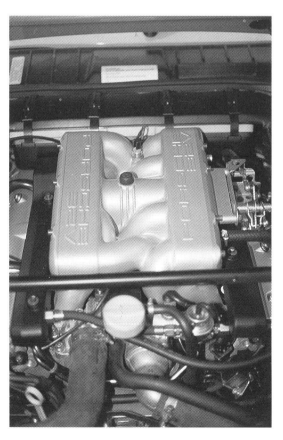

The 928 GT's 32-valve, quad-cam V8 fills the engine bay and delivers a redoubtable 330bhp.

Unmistakably 928 S4: the prominent tailgate spoiler signifies the GT.

The 928 GT offers one of the finest driving environments ever conceived. Seats, driving position and instruments are close to perfection.

Beautifully sculpted 'occasional' rear seats in the 928 GT are better folded down to provide more luggage space.

One area in which the 928 GT apes the 944 S2 is in its wheels – the classically simple seven-spoke design.

Controls to the right of the 928 GT's driver's seat comprise handbrake, remote tailgate release, headlight height adjuster and powered seat adjustment controls.

The 924 was Porsche's first-front engined, water-cooled car. Unloved by some it was certainly controversial.

The basic nose treatment of the 924 (foreground) is similar to the 944's but the overall effect is much daintier. The 944 has broader shoulders and a stockier stance.

One of the 924's more immediately
appealing features is its practicality. The
wrap-around glass tailgate covers a
reasonably sized luggage floor and also
helps rearward visibility.

(Inset) It's easy to see how the 924 might
have been an Audi coupé. Its lines are
light, rounded and fairly aggressive.

The 928 S4 is easier to spot from behind than in front. Larger wrap-around tail lights and modest tailgate spoiler are the clues.

The 928 is a big, heavy car though seldom feels it to drive. But it isn't the easiest of cars to place – the bulbous nose falls away from the driver's line of sight.

The 944's blistered wheelarches allowed the fitment of wider wheels and tyres – but at some cost to aerodynamic efficiency.

The 944's distinctive under-valance spoiler was introduced with the first 16-valve car, the 944 S, and has survived right through to the 968.

The 944 Cabriolet is widely hailed as one of the best looking convertibles of recent years.

THE 944S

G348 YJB

The 944's deep chin spoiler incorporates powerful integral driving lights.

The fully up-dated 944,
called the 968, went on
sale in the UK in the
spring of 1992. Elements
of its styling, by Porsche
design chief Harm
Lagaay, are strongly
reminiscent of 928.

The 944's replacement, the
968, uses recessed
headlights that flip up
when switched on – just
like the 928's.

(Opposite) The 944
Cabriolet was styled by
Tony Lapine. The snug-
fitting hood is fully
powered but the rear cover
has to be unbuttoned by
hand.

The 968 Cabriolet took
over where the 944
Cabriolet left off.
Highlights are its powered
hood and amazing
bodyshell stiffness.

Perhaps the only
questionable aspect of the
968 Cabriolet's styling is
its curiously fluted 'tea-
tray' boot lid.

	Output kW (bhp)	Displacement cc	Output per litre kW (bhp)/l
Porsche 928 GT	243 (330)	4,957	49.0/66.5
Porsche Carrera 2	184 (250)	3,600	51.1/69.4
Ferrari 328 GTB	198 (270)	3,185	62.3/84.8
Ferrari 348 TB	220 (300)	3,405	64.6/88.1
Ferrari Testarossa	287 (390)	4,942	58.1/78.9
Lamborghini Countach	246 (335)	5,167	47.6/64.8
BMW M5	232 (315)	3,535	65.6/89.1

Enough, despite the hefty 3,571lb kerb weight, to push it to 62mph (100km/h) in 5.7secs and on to a top speed of 171mph (275km/h), according to the factory. The GTS will also be the last 928, and is likely to be succeeded by a brand new four-seater before the middle of the decade.

The 928 almost looks better in cutaway form than in the metal. Note all-alloy V8, transaxle transmission and sophisticated Weissach rear axle.

3 944: Plugging the Gap

Porsche's range of front-engined cars was out of balance: the 924, while affordable, had Audi overtones and the 928 was too expensive to appeal to anyone not comfortable carrying platinum plastic. What the company needed was an optimum model to plug the gap and flesh out its line up. Although some felt that the gap ripe for plugging was between the regular 924 and the rapid 924 Turbo, this was only a side issue. Porsche's abiding motive was to distance the new model from the Audi-engined 924 – to make it a *real* Porsche with a *real* Porsche engine. The brief sounded easy enough but, in reality, designing the in-between car turned out to be a fiendishly difficult juggling act.

ENGINE

It was agreed from the start – 1977 was the official project inception year – that the key to the 944's success would be its engine. Unlike the 924's brawny but essentially humdrum powerplant which owed its elevated status under the bonnet of a Porsche to expediency and cost-paring, the 944's unit would have to be genuinely special, a facet of the car's make-up that would generate interest and excitement by itself. In other words, a selling point.

The simplistic interpretation of the 944's creation has Porsche slicing the 928's V8 in half to avail itself of a compact, all-alloy 2.5-litre slant four and installing it in a grown-up version of the 924's bodyshell with broad

shoulders and haunches, better suspension and fatter wheels and tyres. Hey presto! One 944. Well, that's how it looks, doesn't it? But nothing is that simple, of course, least of all the engine that eventually made it into the 944. In the usual Zuffenhausen fashion, Porsche's Weissach-based engineers did not wait for divine inspiration to guide them, but embarked on the laborious task of acquiring various configurations of powerplant and trying them out in prototypes. A straight six was rejected early on as being simply too long to fit into the engine bay, but the idea of a V6 – possibly the 928's V8 with a couple of cylinders lopped off – received much more serious consideration. As an experiment, Porsche's technicians fitted a Peugeot–Renault–Volvo V6 into a 924 chassis with encouraging results.

But in the end, and despite the prestige-related attractions of the multi-cylinder argument, four cylinders won through. First because the size was right: the engine bay of the 924 would not have to be substantially re-worked. Second because with Mitsubishi-style twin balancer shafts – located at different heights on both sides of the cylinder block to balance the second-order vibrations common to all in-line four cylinder engines – it could be made to spin much more smoothly than a conventional four. And third because the proposed capacity of 2.5 litres (and potential for expansion to 2.7 litres and beyond) would make the target 160–200bhp relatively easy to achieve.

The 2.5-litre starter capacity also gives

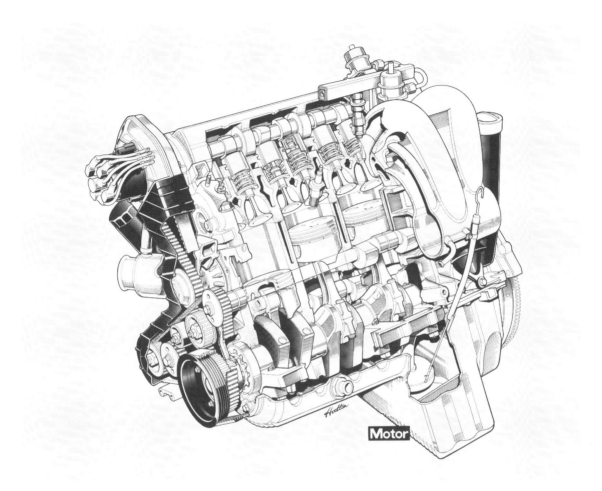

The 944's 'slant four' with balancer shafts would go on to form the basis for half of the 928's V8.

the clue to a somewhat more involved scenario than Porsche chopping a 928 engine in half. As the 928's V8 was then only 4.5 litres, such an exercise would have resulted in a single overhead cam four-cylinder unit of 2.25 litres – rather smaller than Porsche had in mind for its particular power and economy requirements. Increasing the capacity to 2.5 litres by stretching the bore was one obvious solution and, in the event, the one that was chosen. But it was not ideal, giving very oversquare bore/stroke dimensions of 100/78.9mm, an arrangement

generally reckoned to be less than ideal for good economy. Lengthening the stroke, however, was out of the question since this would have made the engine too tall. As it was it had to be canted over at 30 degrees to clear the bonnet line.

Engine Construction

In its construction, however, the new four had strong parallels with the V8. Both the cylinder head and crankcase/cylinder block were made from aluminium alloy, the latter

Cutaway of 944 shows same basic front engine/rear gearbox layout as 924 but Porsche-designed engine is bigger, body broader, brakes beefier, wheels and tyres wider.

being a particularly beefy casting with prominent strengthening ribs. Of open deck configuration, it had no liners as such but, instead, the skirts of the alloy pistons were chromed to mate with bores with high-silicon friction-bearing surfaces thanks to a type of aluminium developed by Reynolds Aluminium of bicycle frame fame. The crankcase was a one-piece ladder-type casting and incorporated all the caps for a substantial forged steel crankshaft running in five main bearings. Made from sintered steel for extra strength and lightness, the con rods carried fully floating gudgeon pins.

The crank provided direct drive for a

crescent-type oil pump at the front of the shaft and, via two toothed rubber belts, the water pump and counterbalance shafts. Outboard of this was a multi-vee belt for the alternator. Nothing unusual about that. Far more ingenious was the combined water/oil intercooler on the right side of the block which, by allowing heat to be dissipated between the two liquids, speeded the warm-up of the oil from a cold start and kept it at the right temperature (a little below the boiling point of water) in hard driving.

Located by a couple of dowels and secured by ten long bolts, the cylinder head was, in all important respects, pure 928 – albeit

The 944's beauty is more than skin deep. Fully galvanised body carries a ten-year warranty against perforations.

with a slightly modified combustion chamber shape. As with the 928, the valves were orientated in-line, two per cylinder, but inclined slightly from the bore centre line. These were set in an inclined wedge-shaped combustion chamber not quite as wide as the cylinder bore and therefore bound to create squish where the pistons overlapped. The resulting enhanced turbulence within the combustion chamber enabled the use of both a high (10.6:1) compression ratio and a lean part-throttle mixture, promising good response and economy.

A further benefit in this area was Porsche's adoption of fully electronic control for both ignition advance and fuel injection – to wit Bosch Motronic breakerless ignition and Bosch L-Jetronic injection. Thus equipped, the 944's engine developed 163bhp at 5,800rpm and 151lb ft of torque at 3,000rpm. Peak power compared with 125bhp for the normally aspirated 2-litre 924 and 177 and 210bhp respectively for the 924 Turbo and Carrera GTS.

TRANSMISSION, CHASSIS AND STYLING

For use in the 944, the 924's five-speed

944 (1982)

Engine
Longitudinal, front, rear-wheel drive
Capacity	2,479cc, 4-cyl in-line (2,681cc with new block in 1989)
Bore/Stroke	100/79mm (104/79mm 1989)
Compression ratio	10.6:1 (10.9:1 1989)
Head/Block	Al alloy/Al alloy
Valve gear	Sohc, 2 valves per cylinder
Fuel and Ignition	Electronic ignition, Bosch Motronic fuel injection and engine management
Max Power	163bhp at 5,800rpm (165bhp/5,800rpm 1989)
Max Torque	151lb ft at 3,500rpm (166lb ft/4,200rpm, 1989)

Gearbox
Five-speed manual or three-speed automatic

Suspension
Front	Independent, single wishbones, MacPherson struts, coil springs, telescopic dampers, anti-roll bar
Rear	Independent, semi-trailing arms, transverse torsion bars, coil springs, telescopic dampers, anti-roll bar

Steering
Rack and pinion, power assistance on later models

Brakes
Front	Ventilated discs
Rear	Ventilated discs
ABS	Not available until 1987

Wheels and Tyres
Cast alloy, 7×15in, 185/70 VR15 tyres, 7×16in wheels with 205/55 VR16 tyres optional

Dimensions
Length	165in (4,200mm)
Width	68.3in (1,735mm)
Height	50.2in (1,275mm)
Weight	2,600lb (1,267kg)

transmission (three-speed automatic optional) was strengthened to cope with the higher outputs and made good use of slightly higher ratios. The new car's chassis took its cues from the 924 Carrera GT's, using similar rack and pinion steering but revised settings for the strut front/semi-trailing arm rear suspension and with stronger semi-trailing arms, meaty front and rear anti-roll bars and a 1.8in (46mm) longer wheelbase. And as with the suspension so with the brakes: ventilated discs front and rear *à la* Carrera. The similarity even extended to the styling, the 944 sharing the fastest 924's bulging arches, though these were now an integral part of the galvanized steel body rather than tacked on polyurethane items: still plastic, though, was the deep chin spoiler. Beneath the broader shoulders nestled wider wheels and tyres – 185/70VR 15 Pirelli CN36s on 7×15in with 215/60s as a cost option and one which most customers went for, if only on aesthetic grounds.

Those expecting a transformation on the inside, however, were to be disappointed. But for a rather better quality of fabric trim and carpeting, the fitting of a 911-style three-spoke steering wheel and some (invisible) tweaking of the 924's mediocre heating and ventilation system, the cabins were all but identical. What criticisms the motoring press had of the 944 were directed here, most commentators singling out the drab instruments, low-wheeled driving position and poor suppression of road noise for a moan. Otherwise, media reaction to the 'pumped-up 924' were extremely positive, especially over the performance.

RECEPTION

In its 1982 road test, *Motor* decided that its 944 Lux test car was too rapid to risk flat out through MIRA's viciously tight banked turns but did manage to record 135mph (217km/h) in opposite directions and was happy to give Porsche's 137mph (220km/h) top speed claim the nod. The testers experienced no difficulty in bettering the factory's acceleration figures, though, launching the 944 to 60mph (0–96km/h) in 7.2secs and on to 100mph (160km/h) in 20.1secs, concluding that, from a standing start at least, the new Porsche had the measure of most of its rivals. But energetic sprinter as the 944 was

from a standing start, it did its best work on the move. Then those big pots really let loose.

To quote from the test:

It's the fourth and fifth gear times that most clearly illustrate the way the 944 goes on the road. Between 20 and 90mph in fourth, for example, the successive 20mph speed increments occupy just 6.6, 6.2, 6.0, 6.0, 6.1 and 6.7 seconds respectively, clear evidence of the new engine's flat, meaty torque curve. In combination with instantaneous throttle response, the result is the deep-chested, almost casual performance of a much larger engine with up to twice as many cylinders; and it's an impression that is heavily underlined by the 944's mechanical refinement.

So sweetly does the engine spin throughout its rev range that Porsche hardly do it justice in claiming it to be as smooth as a good 'six': we'd say that its freedom from vibration can stand comparison with a good V8. The engine revs so freely and with such a silken, well-bred sound that the protective ignition cut-out is really needed to prevent you inadvertently exceeding the 6,500rpm rev limit, and subjectively it seems even quieter than the moderate 81dBA we recorded at peak revs in second gear.

All that and respectable fuel efficiency, too. In *Motor*'s hands, the 944 returned what the magazine could only describe as an 'astonishing' 24.8mpg (11.4l/100km) overall, some 2–3mpg clear than even the most parsimonious of its rivals. Also awarded high marks were the well-spaced gear ratios – allowing speeds of 34, 58, 85 and 115mph (55, 93, 137 and 185km/h) at 6,500rpm in the first four gears – though the gearchange

The 944 Cabriolet: capable of putting the wind through your hair at 145mph (233km/h).

The 3-litre, 16-valve 944S2 engine is a real powerhouse – it has a very flat torque curve, peaking at 4,000rpm with 207lb ft. This one belongs to a Cabriolet.

Nose treatment of the 944 was tidied for the S2 and looks far more 'all-of-a-piece'. Note the neatly integrated driving lights.

This smooth, seven-spoke style alloy wheel replaced the familiar 'phone-dial' design on the 944.

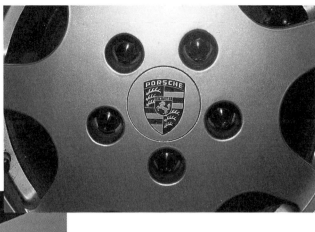

The 944 door mirrors place the field of vision ahead of Cd.

This 944 Cabriolet's cabin isn't finished in the most practical of colours but there's no doubting its comfort. Seat shaping and driving position are superb.

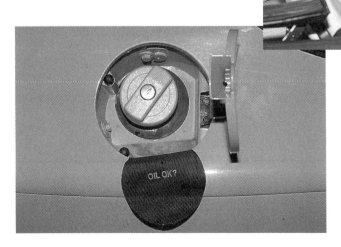

Typical Porsche thoroughness: not only a flap to catch petrol drips but a reminder to check the oil.

itself was censured for being a shade notch, especially between 1st and 2nd.

HANDLING AND RIDE

The quality of the handling attracted no such negativism. On the contrary, it received universal approbation for its combination of high grip and superb balance on the limit. Here was a car that could be exploited by even the moderately skilled, yet not frighten the unsuspecting. This is what *Autocar* said:

> There is plenty of suspension movement, yet the car rolls very little when cornered hard – a factor that inspires confidence, as does the car's ultimate cornering behaviour. Perhaps because of the longer wheelbase, it is an easier car to drive consistently fast than the 924 Carrera was. No wet conditions were encountered, but on dry surfaces there is a reassuring degree of understeer. Ease gently off the throttle, and the car goes 'neutral' while an abrupt lift off in mid bend will cause the tail to gently move out a little, a situation which allows the driver to create the state of balance he likes without fear of the car biting back.

A firm and sometimes choppy ride was not so well received but, in many ways, the big news about the 944 had already been told. Here was an extremely successful marriage of style, power and poise that lifted the model clear of the 924 in all its forms, even the potent Carrera.

CABIN

The inside story, however, was much the same, the 944's cabin looking all but identical to the 924's. For the most part, this was no bad thing as it meant bags of front legroom, well shaped seats and a basically well thought out driving position. The latter was somewhat marred by the low set, non-adjustable steering wheel and dimly marked instruments, but the spacing of the pedals and siting of the minor switchgear were fine.

It was probably *Motor* that best captured the significance of the new car:

> In summarizing the 944 it's easy enough to predict that even judged solely as a sports car – as a finely honed driving machine in the traditional Porsche mould – its commercial success is assured. But the real significance of the 944 goes much deeper than that. The true measure of Porsche's achievement is that these sporting virtues have been built into a package that also attains new levels of social acceptability for a high performance motor car. At the heart of the 944 is a sensationally smooth and civilized engine which endows it with fuel economy to make the oil moguls weep in their oil barrels. With total tractability, a seven year anti-corrosion warranty and 12,000-mile oil change intervals as icing on the cake, the socially responsible 944 owner can enjoy his motoring with a conscience as pure as the driven snow.

944 TURBO

True enough, plenty of people wanted to become 944 owners. Within a year of its launch, the 944's star had completely eclipsed the 924's, the newcomer accounting for over half of total Porsche sales. But that was not the end of the story – far from it. In 1983, in an effort to get the 944's interior looking more up-market than the 924's, it

The 944 Turbo was unveiled in February, 1985. Developing 220bhp, its performance was a match for a normally aspirated 911's.

was re-trimmed in a vastly smarter pin-stripe fabric. To reinforce the enhanced elegance, a new design of alloy road wheel was also introduced. This, however, was a mere hair-combing exercise compared to major workout scheduled for 1985 and the debut of the Turbo.

With this car, Porsche really had set the cat among the pigeons. After my first drive, I was convinced that it was the finest car the Stuttgart-based company had ever made. As fast as a 911 Carrera, as roomy as a 928S and more fuel-efficient than either, it truly qualified as a Porsche great and a formidable performance package by any standards.

From the very beginning of the normally aspirated 944's development, a turbo-charged version was planned, just as it had

been with the 924. The first clue to the nature of the new car came in 1981 when a 924 GTP driven by Walter Rohrl and Jurgen Barth finished 7th at Le Mans. That car, powered by a new turbocharged 2.5-litre in-line 'four' was none other than a prototype racer for the road-going 944 Turbo. As well as whipping numerous more powerful rivals in the famous endurance event, it bagged a number of technical firsts.

Most significantly, Porsche combined fully electronic ignition with a timed fuel injection system, so that the ignition advance and the amount of fuel injected were controlled according to the engine speed and load by a computer which integrated signals from sensors monitoring turbo boost pressure, air intake temperature and engine speed. If

944 Turbo (1985)

Engine
Longitudinal, front, rear-wheel drive

Capacity	2,497cc, 4-cyl in-line
Bore/Stroke	100/79mm
Compression ratio	8.0:1
Head/Block	Al alloy/Al alloy
Valve gear	Sohc, 2 valves per cylinder
Fuel and Ignition	Electronic ignition, Bosch Motronic fuel injection and engine management with knock sensor. KKK turbocharger, intercooler
Max Power	220bhp at 5,800rpm
Max Torque	243lb ft at 3,500rpm

Gearbox
Five-speed manual or three-speed automatic

Suspension

Front	Independent, single wishbones, MacPherson struts, coil springs, telescopic dampers, anti-roll bar
Rear	Independent, semi-trailing arms, transverse torsion bars, coil springs, telescopic dampers, anti-roll bar

Steering
Rack and pinion, power assistance

Brakes

Front	Ventilated discs
Rear	Ventilated discs
ABS	Optional

Wheels and Tyres
Cast alloy, 7×16in, (front), 8×16in (rear), 205/55 VR16 (front), 225/50 VR16 tyres (rear)

Dimensions

Length	165in (4,200mm)
Width	68.3in (1,735mm)
Height	50.2in (1,275mm)
Weight	2,600lb (1,267kg)

reliability can be defined as spending least time in the pits, the Porsche was the most reliable car in the field.

A pukka pre-production 944 Turbo was not seen until June 1984 when one competed in the 24-hour Nelson Ledges race at Ohio, USA. The car was driven by Freddy Baker, Jim Busby and Rick Knoop and it won the race by an emphatic 42 laps. In an event where all the competing cars had to be fitted with catalytic converters, the Porsche's victory was perhaps less of a surprise than some commentators were suggesting. From the very start, Porsche had set out to design a car that would develop the same power with a 'cat' as without. The 944 Turbo met that brief. And many others. Improvements over the normally aspirated 944 were sought in four major areas: engine, chassis, bodywork and cabin. Several of the interior and chassis changes were to become standardized throughout the 944 range, but not the turbocharged version of the 944's already brawny 2.5-litre, fuel-injected 'four'.

TECHNICAL IMPROVEMENTS

Technical highlights included a new combustion chamber with high turbulence and thermal efficiency. The design depended on a relatively high (8.0:1) compression ratio to maintain good off-boost torque and to guard against detonation, a knock sensor was incorporated as part of the engine management system. This, as with the normally aspirated 944, was based around the Bosch Motronic injection/ignition which used an engine map with 256 fixed points in its programmable fixed value memory to meet the particular operating needs of the turbo engine.

Temperature management embraced water cooling for the KKK Type K26 turbocharger (maximum boost 11psi) and an intercooler to lower the temperature of the charge intake air. An external oil cooler saw to the engine's operating temperatures. Even a casual analysis of the new power and torque outputs was enough to convince sceptics that this car would obliterate associations between modest performance and the Porsche's pretty, 924-derived profile for good. A hike of 35 per cent took peak power up to 220bhp at 5,800rpm while, at 243lb ft,

the turbo powerplant developed some 40lb ft more than the 911 Carrera's normally aspirated 3.2-litre flat six.

PERFORMANCE

Naturally, the 944's performance was transformed. *Motor*'s subsequent road test recorded a top speed of 158mph (254km/h) and 0–60mph (0–96km/h) in 5.9secs – exceptional figures both. This is what the magazine's testers had to say:

> In normal driving, the 944 Turbo can be a sublimely docile machine, responsive but velvet-gloved in its power delivery. The engine's off-boost tameness – apparent below about 2,500rpm in any gear – shouldn't be confused with turbo lag. Inevitably there is some but, when pushing hard, it's of little consequence. Of more significance is a throttle action that unleashes the power very gently and progressively over the first 98 per cent of its travel, saving a useful measure of explosive urgency for full depression. This is clearly a sensible if unusual arrangement, allowing brisk yet economical progress in all circumstances save those rare occasions where maximum acceleration is called for – most notably when overtaking.

The Turbo's transaxle drivetrain was carried over from the regular 944 but, to cope with the extra power, it received a bigger clutch with high-friction face material and a stronger five-speed gearbox. Bodywork changes were nothing if not subtle, the new, smoothly contoured nose section incorporating cooling ducts for engine and brakes as well as integral, high-intensity fog lamps and indicators. Together with the flush windscreen, flared sills, a re-shaped tail

The 944 Turbo's rear valance spoiler and rear-end styling improve airflow management at speed.

Not especially big by Porsche standards, the Turbo's tailgate spoiler is nevertheless generously proportioned for a 944.

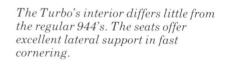

The Turbo's interior differs little from the regular 944's. The seats offer excellent lateral support in fast cornering.

The 944 Turbo's engine is distinguished by its distinctive plumbing.

spoiler and the addition of an under-bumper aerofoil which contributed to smoother air-flow management under the car, it helped lower the Cd from 0.35 to 0.33.

Under the smoother skin, the standard car's floating caliper brakes had been replaced by more efficient, four-piston, fixed caliper units with heat-resistant aluminium alloy housings. Front and rear suspension arms, previously made from welded sheet metal, were manufactured in cast aluminium for the Turbo. Unsurprisingly, both springs and dampers were re-rated for the new car and the 'phone-dial' style cast aluminium wheels made familiar by the 928 became standard, as did power steering.

Cabin alterations stretched to a new facia which combined 928-style dials with 911-style shaping, revised switchgear, electric height and rake adjustment for the front seats and a more sophisticated heating and ventilation system.

As already established, the Turbo was blistering in a straight line, but could the chassis handle the extra power? The answer was plain after a brief drive in the South of France where Porsche held the car's international launch. I filed my findings for *Motor*:

There's understeer to be sure, but only to a degree that settles the car when entering a bend; it's never excessive. Grip is simply tremendous and matched with unflappable stability over bumps. The car jiggles, the tyres thump, but the line is held with an iron will. In bends, the steering weighs up nicely and inspires plenty of confidence at the helm. It's a little too light about the straight ahead, however, a characteristic that can make the front wheels feel somewhat remote at speed.

ROAD TEST

Reproduced from *Motor*
Road Tests Annual 1985

PORSCHE 944 TURBO

Like a good storyteller's innate ability to spin out a simple plot while retaining the listeners' undivided attention, Porsche has mastered the similarly difficult knack of stretching an old design over the span of decades while increasing its popularity.

No better example exists of this philosophy than the seemingly immortal 911 – a design which can, almost incredibly, trace its roots back to the Beetle-esque flat-four engined 356 yet which today, as the 911 Turbo, is widely acknowledged as not only one of the very quickest of the world's supercars but also one of the most practical and useable day-to-day. And this in spite of a rear-engined chassis configuration that, by all rights, should have been dead and buried before Neil Armstrong set foot upon the moon in the late 'Sixties. At Porsche, conventional wisdom is viewed with acid scepticism.

Presented with such clear evidence that inspired development can conquer all it is, perhaps, surprising that so many advocates of the Stuttgart-Zuffenhausen-based marque felt betrayed when the company introduced the humble 924 in 1971. Conceived by Porsche as a classy VW–Audi front-engined sports coupé – but sold back to Porsche when VW ran into financial problems – the 924 was critically regarded as the runt of a proven pack. Understandably so. Although dynamically more accomplished than any road car Porsche had hitherto produced and sold at (by Porsche standards) a budget price, it entirely lacked the excitement, build quality and charisma of the older design. Porsche die-hards devoutly wished it had remained an Audi, but they should have known better. For in just 14 years – a little over half the time it took the first 911 to become the car it is today – the 924 has itself become a respectable Porsche, while spawning a succession of developments culminating in what must be regarded as the most significant Porsche for years. The 944 Turbo.

Significant because the latest car in the 920 line is the first viable alternative to the 911. If the 2.5-litre-engined 944 was devised to plug the gap between the 924 and 911 – something which two versions of the 924 Turbo singularly failed to do – there can be no doubt where the 944 Turbo sits: right in the 911 Carrera's lap. When the new car goes on sale in the UK towards the end of the year it is expected to cost between £25,000 and £27,000. That compares with a current price of £25,277 for the Carrera. The turbo-car's arrival is likely to stir up more than a little controversy and heart-searching, despite Porsche's contention that it will appeal to a different sort of buyer than the 911 traditionalist. We suspect that Porsche's argument is more intuitive than rational, since with two such diverse designs, chasing the same performance/dynamic/value goals, only one can represent the best buy as perceived by Porsche and its customers. As intrigued as any 911 fans to know which is the better car, we flew to Germany with our test gear to find out, picking up a 944 Turbo at Stuttgart Airport and driving it hard for two days: flat out along autobahns, entertainingly through the Black Forest, in convoy with swift 911s. At the end of it we had all the figures we needed. We also had an answer.

The 944 Turbo has been fully described in a previous feature, but it's worth reviewing the salient points here. Several of the changes introduced with the Turbo at its February launch (improved suspension arm castings and cabin design) have since been adopted as running modifications to the normally-aspirated 944, but the more muscular engine of the new car is clearly the focus of interest.

The 944's deep-chested all-alloy 2479 cc 'four', with its contra-rotating balancer shafts, is a world removed from the 924's ex-VW van engine and it comes as no surprise that, in various guises, it will soon be the only engine available in 920-series cars.

The turbo motor is the same two valves-per-cylinder design, but with a lower compression ratio (8.0 instead of 10.6 to 1) to accommodate the forced induction created by an intercooled KKK turbocharger. Engine management is provided by a knock sensor and a modified Bosch Motronic 'black box' which monitors a variety of running parameters like engine speed, boost pressure (wastage-limited to a maximum of 11 psi), inlet manifold temperature and throttle opening and, in so doing, adjusts fuel feed, ignition timing and exhaust emissions to maintain optimum efficiency. The Motronic system also gives cold-start enrichment and, at the other end of the scale, fuel feed cut-off on a trailing throttle. A larger alternator and radiator and an external oil cooler are exclusively part of the turbo engine's specification, too. Maximum power is 200 bhp at 5800 rpm (10 down on the Carrera's 3.2-litre flat six at 100 revs less) with a hefty 243 lb ft of torque at 3500 rpm (203 lb ft at 4800 rpm for the 911). For markets where the 944 Turbo is fitted with a power-sapping emissions catalytic converter Porsche merely re-program the Motronic system and hike the turbo boost pressure: the figures remain the same.

In common with the 924, 928, normally-aspirated 944 and, indeed, future all-wheel drive variations of the 911, the Turbo's five-speed gearbox is mounted at the opposite end of the driveshaft to the engine in unit with the final drive, but is uprated to cope with the more powerful engine and has longer gear ratios. Suspension is also modified, with redesigned transverse links cast in aluminium rather than pressed out of sheet steel and re-rated springs and dampers. The front MacPherson struts get an anti-roll bar to

The elegant styling of the 944 Turbo.

match the one at the semi-trailing arm torsion bar-sprung rear. Further chassis changes include standard power assistance for the rack and pinion steering, four-pot fixed calipers for the front and rear discs and fatter tyres (205/55VR16 front, 225/50VR16 rear) for the new 'phone dial' style alloy wheels.

Body changes are subtle but telling. The Turbo's nose section features a reshaped bumper and a new spoiler with integral driving lamps. At the rear, however, there is a physical addition in the shape of an apron spoiler which is said to improve directional stability by reducing rear lift. It also helps reduce the drag factor by a point to an impressive 0.33.

Inside, the improvements are more immediately apparent. Ditched are the old steering wheel, instruments/facia and Porsche-designed front seats, replaced by genuine Recaros with electrically-powered height adjustment, a new and repositioned four-spoke steering wheel, clearer 928-style instruments and a more elegantly fashioned facia incorporating larger air outlets and

With 250bhp, the 944 Turbo has as much performance as normally aspirated 911s. Over 150mph (241km/h) and 0–60mph (0–96km/h) in around five and a half seconds.

revised heating and ventilation controls. Better-looking door panels and a restyled centre console are also part of the new interior deal. Exactly how much equipment UK-spec cars will carry is still unknown to us but it seems certain they will have the power windows, heated windscreen and headlamp washers and four-speaker stereo system fitted to our German-registered test car.

Even if Porsche decided to leave it at that for the UK-export model, the 944 Turbo would carry at least as much showroom appeal as the Carrera. But if, in the ensuing months, the launch price creeps closer to the £27,000 mark, queueing customers should expect a plusher package with maybe even air conditioning included as standard. Either way, the 944 Turbo will be judged by the standards of the junior supercar class. If you're in the market for high-priced excitement, there's no lack of talent. Home-grown challengers include Jaguar's *XJS HE* (£23,995) and the Lotus Esprit Turbo

(£22,760) while, from Italy, Ferrari fields the 308 GTB Quattrovalvole (£29,100) and Lamborghini Jalpa 350 (£28,450). Four-wheel drive handling and grip is represented by the Audi Quattro (£22,616). But as already hinted at the 944 Turbo's greatest rival comes from the same stable in the shape of the £25,277 911 Carrera which, on paper at least, should have the edge in straight-line performance.

And so it is in practice, but the 911's advantage is confined to standing start acceleration. Flat out on the autobahn, the 944 Turbo recorded a remarkable two-way maximum of 157.9 mph, which is not only 5 mph better than Porsche's claim but also nearly 7 mph faster than the 911 Carrera could manage when we tested it in 1984. Of the rivals we've maximum speed tested, none is faster.

The factory's acceleration claims were harder to beat but, even so, our test car shaved a few tenths off the benchmark times, reaching 60 mph from rest in 5.9 sec and 100 mph in 14.8 sec. These figures are clearly a class removed from what the normally-aspirated 944 is capable of (7.2/20.1 sec) if not a match for the Carrera's 5.3 and 13.6 sec or the 308 QV's 5.7 and 14.3 sec. But, as the figures show, it's a very close thing and there can be no question that the Turbo has joined the ranks of the super sprinters.

In fourth and fifth gears – a better indication of how a car performs on the road – the 944 Turbo more obviously exhibits turbo characteristics with relatively weak engine response at low revs, building to storming mid-range urge which is well maintained to the 6400 rpm red line. In fifth, for example, the 20–40 and 30–50 mph times of 13.6 and 11.8 sec respectively look decidedly limp-wristed, but by the time the engine is benefiting from maximum turbo boost and can bring the full weight of its considerable mid-range torque to bear the increment times fall dramatically. Between 60 and 110 mph no single 20 mph increment takes more than 7.6

sec while 60–80 mph is disposed of in just 6.9 sec. Apply the same test to the shorter-geared Carrera and it's not even in the same race, taking 9.9 sec to cover the 90–110 mph increment the 944 Turbo despatched in 7.6 sec and 8.5 sec for 60–80 mph. The message is clear: once the 944 Turbo gets moving in the upper speed ranges, there's little this side of a full-blown exotic that can live with it.

Yet in normal driving it can be a sublimely docile machine, responsive but velvet-gloved in its power delivery. The engine's off-boost tameness – apparent below about 2500 rpm in any gear – shouldn't be confused with turbo lag. Inevitably there is some but, when pushing hard, it's of little consequence. Of more significance is a throttle action that unleashes the power very gently and progressively over the first 98 per cent of its travel, saving a useful measure of explosive urgency for full depression. This is clearly a sensible if unusual arrangement, allowing brisk yet economical progress in all circumstances save those rare occasions where maximum acceleration is called for – most notably when overtaking.

If the Turbo's throttle characteristics set it at odds with its normally-aspirated namesake (a car noted for its punchy, eager part-throttle response) the quality of its engine note is no less dissimilar. The silky smoothness is still there but disguised to a large extent by an underlying gruffness not apparent in the ordinary 944. It's an aggressive well-bred sound not out of keeping with the performance image of the car though, subjectively, it seems louder than the modest 80 dBA we recorded at peak revs in second gear.

It would be hard to imagine even the most enthusiastic 944 Turbo owner driving his car harder than we did our test car over two days and 500 miles, so take it as read that the 22.5 mpg we logged overall is a conservative result. But it's nothing less than a remarkable one: even the much slower non-turbo

944 could manage no better than 24.8 mpg tested over twice the mileage and, of our selected rivals, it is predictably only the 911 Carrera (21.1 mpg) that gets closer. With its enlarged 17.7-gallon (80-litre) tank brimmed with 4-star, the 944 Turbo should thus be good for at least 380 miles between refills, well over 400 miles with a little restraint.

As with the ordinary 944, the Turbo's gearchange is no marvel of precision or slickness but it is both positive and consistent with good spring loading to the 3/4 plane. The Turbo's lower final drive ratio (3.37 against 3.89) means longer overall gearing though the intermediate ratios – which give maxima of 39, 66, 97 and 132 mph at 6400 rpm – remain progressively stacked and at 70 mph in fifth (25.8 mph/1000 rpm) the engine is turning over at a lazy 2700 rpm. The clutch has a long travel, but is well cushioned without being too heavy.

The ordinary 944 is a dogged understeerer. The 944 Turbo is not. Assymetrically-sized tyres front-to-rear, revised spring and damper settings and a 35 per cent power increase to the rear wheels all conspire to make it a far more neutrally-balanced and entertaining machine. Grip and traction are still the car's strong suits, but the changes have literally opened up new horizons for the driver should he want to exploit them.

It would be hard to imagine power steering any better than this car's. The assistance plays a supporting role to response, accuracy and informative feedback – as it should do – but the driver needs to exert no great effort at the helm when parking. In fact it's a sense of effortlessness and calm control that the driver is most aware of when conducting the car briskly, too. There's masses of grip and quick, accurately obedient turn-in to rely on at all times and, in most circumstances, the rear tyres stick to the tarmac like marmalade to a blanket. But the understeer is initial, a transient phase leading to a gloriously long period of neutrality where the chassis is at its

best, lucidly responding to subtle inputs and flicks. Pushed harder still on fast sweeps there is oversteer; not manifested as a warning of impending doom but as a gentle reminder that faster cornering will be wasted as tyre scrub. Its onset is slow and progressive, easily controlled with just a nudge of corrective lock.

More oversteer is readily available to the extrovert driver but he must brake deep into a corner to get it. Then the tail will swing out in a pendulous slide that requires an armful of opposite lock and a bootful of power to stabilise and hold. The results, if unnecessary, are spectacular and a telling testimony to the 944 Turbo's terrific balance and poise. Try the same thing in a 911 and you'd have to be either extremely good or extremely lucky not to spin. Merely lifting off mid-bend in the Turbo induces pronounced tuck-in which remains the safe side of oversteer and is useful for adjusting the car's line through a bend.

Nor will the Porsche's line be upset by bumps. As with its less powerful counterpart, suspension control is exemplary, a virtue which has the added benefit of keeping body motion tightly in check. Where the 944 Turbo steps into a class of its own, however, is with the quality of its ride. It remains firm but never jarringly so; small bumps and ridges are more successfully smothered, motorway undulations more successfully flattened. Braking is immensely powerful but still displays the annoying trait of not feathering off smoothly with gentle 'check' applications of the otherwise firm and progressive pedal.

The combination of raising the steering wheel by half an inch and fitting slimmer yet more shapely Recaro front seats with height adjustment on the driver's side has transformed the Porsche's driving position. As before, there's ample legroom for even the tallest driver, but you no longer sit with the wheel in your lap. The new 911-style stalks are also more pleasant to use than the ex-VW

PERFORMANCE

Performance tests carried out by *Motor's* staff on the Continent.

WEATHER CONDITIONS

Wind	0–7mph
Temperature	72 deg F/22 deg C
Barometer	29.7 in Hg/1006 mbar
Surface	Dry tarmacadam

MAXIMUM SPEEDS

	mph	kph
Max. Speed (in fifth gear)	157.9	254.1
Terminal Speeds:		
at ¼ mile	99	159
at kilometre	129	207
Speed in gears (at 6400rpm):		
1st	39	63
2nd	66	106
3rd	97	156
4th	132	212

ACCELERATION FROM REST

mph	sec	kph	sec
0–30	2.3	0–40	1.9
0–40	3.4	0–60	3.0
0–50	4.5	0–80	4.6
0–60	5.9	0–100	6.3
0–70	7.8	0–120	8.8
0–80	9.8	0–140	11.3
0–90	11.9	0–160	14.8
0–100	14.9	0–180	19.2
0–110	18.1	0–200	24.5
0–120	22.2		
0–130	26.9		
Standing ¼	14.5	Standing km	26.2

ACCELERATION IN TOP

mph	sec	kph	sec
20–40	13.6	40–60	8.5
30–50	11.8	60–80	7.1
40–60	10.4	80–100	5.7
50–70	8.4	100–120	4.5
60–80	6.9	120–140	4.2
70–90	7.0	140–160	4.8
80–100	7.4	160–180	5.2
90–110	7.6	180–200	6.2
100–120	8.5		
110–130	11.5		

ACCELERATION IN 4TH

mph	sec	kph	sec
20–40	9.0	40–60	5.6
30–50	7.7	60–80	4.4
40–60	6.2	80–100	3.3
50–70	5.2	100–120	3.1
60–80	5.0	120–140	3.1
70–90	5.1	140–160	3.5
80–100	5.4	160–180	4.0
90–110	6.2	180–200	5.6
100–120	7.2		

NOISE

	dBA
30mph	67
50mph	69
70mph	72
Maximum‡	80

‡Peak noise level under full-throttle acceleration in 2nd

STEERING

Turning circle lock to lock	10.4m, 34ft 3.3 turns

FUEL CONSUMPTION

Overall	22.5mpg
	12.5 litres/100km
*Touring	30.2mpg
	9.3 litres/100km
Govt tests	23.0mpg (urban)
	41.5mpg (56mph)
	33.2mpg (75mph)
Fuel grade	97 octane
	4 star rating
Tank capacity	80 litres
	17.7 galls
Max range*	534 miles
	860km
Test distance	487 miles
	783km

*based on official fuel economy figures – 50 per cent of urban cycle, plus 25 per cent of each 56/75mph consumptions

SPEEDOMETER (mph)

True mph	30	40	50	60	70	80	90	100
Speedo	31	42	52	63	73	83	94	104

Distance recorder: 3.3 per cent fast

WEIGHT

	kg	cwt
Unladen weight*	1258	24.8
Weight as tested	1442	28.4

*No fuel

Test Data: World Copyright reserved. No reproduction in whole or part without written permission.

GENERAL SPECIFICATION

ENGINE

Cylinders	4 in-line
Capacity	2479cc
Bore/stroke	100/78.9mm
Max power	220bhp 162KW at 5800rpm (DIN)
Max torque	243lb ft 179 Nm at 3500rpm (DIN)
Block	Aluminium alloy
Head	Aluminium alloy
Cooling	Water
Valve gear	Sohc
Compression	8.0:1
Fuel system	Bosch L-Jetronic fuel injection
Ignition	Bosch Motronic fully programmed
Bearings	5 main

TRANSMISSION

Drive	To rear wheels
Type	5-speed manual
Internal ratios and mph/1000rpm	
Top	0.829:1/25.8
4th	1.034:1/20.7
3rd	1.400:1/15.3
2nd	2.059:1/10.5
1st	3.500:1/6.2
Rev	3.500:1
Final drive	3.37:1

AERODYNAMICS

Coef Cd	0.33

SUSPENSION

Front	Independent by Mac-Pherson struts, lower wishbones, coil springs, anti-roll bar, gas filled dampers
Rear	Independent by semi-trailing arms, torsion bar, anti-roll bar, gas filled dampers

STEERING

Type	Rack and pinion
Assistance	Yes

BRAKES

Type	Ventilated discs, 30cm dia
Rear	Discs, 30cm dia
Servo	Yes
Circuit	Dual, split front rear
Rear valve	No

WHEELS/TYRES

Type	Cast alloy, 7 and 8in × 16in dia
Tyres	205/55 VR 16 (front) 225/50 VR 16 (rear)
Pressures F/R (normal)	29/36 psi 2.0/2.5 bar

ELECTRICAL

Battery	12V, 50Ah
Alternator	115 amp
Fuses	24
Headlights	
type	Halogen
dip	100W total
main	120W total

GUARANTEE

Duration	12 months, unlimited mileage
Rust warranty	6 years

MAINTENANCE

Major service	12,000 miles

Make: Porsche **Model:** 944 Turbo **Country of Origin:** Germany
Maker: Dr Ing hcF Porsche AG, 7000 Stuttgart-Zuffenhausen, Porschestrasse 42, West Germany
UK Concessionaire: Porsche Cars Great Britain Ltd, Richfield Avenue, Reading, Berkshire, RG1 8PH. Tel: (0734) 595411
Total Price: Not yet decided for UK. Expected to be £25,000/£27,000

Golf items of old. In both aesthetic and practical terms, the new facia is a big improvement though not without flaws. The 928-style instruments are cleanly styled and look good but the outer dials (water temperature and battery voltage) are partially obscured by the leather-trimmed wheel rim and, in bright sunlight, the binnacle cowling is insufficiently deep to prevent bad reflections in the bottom half of the display. Likewise, the new electronically controlled heating and ventilation system with its dial-a-temperature facility and four-speed fan looks impressive and, we've no doubt, can supply a mirage-inducing blast of hot air when required. But when the heat-wave is outside – as it was when we tested the car – the plethora of direction and volume-adjustable vents simply aren't up to the task of directing a decent volume of air into the cabin under ram pressure. And the booster fan is unacceptably noisy on the highest of its settings.

The rest is generally good news: fine visibility, superb lighting and wipers, smart and tasteful interior furnishings to match the classy new facia and excellent build quality and exterior finish. The 944 Turbo is by no means the quietest car in the class (there's little to touch an XJS) but it is a more civilised and refined machine than the 911 Carrera.

At the end of the day, it's also the better car, however hard old-school Porsche devotees may find that to accept or believe. In saying this, it's not our intention to deride the older car. The 911 represents a set of strengths and values that will remain appealing for as long as cars have wheels and are powered by internal combustion. The 3.2-litre flat-six is a wonderful power plant: seductively smooth and urgent, as crisp as a metal-flake Granny Smith, bursting with life and charisma. If you're man enough to tame it, the chassis is more rewarding than any other and few would deny the prestige attached to the timeless shape of those three evocative figures:

911. But consider a car that has all of its pace and more, the economy and refinement of a quick family saloon, space in the back for kids, and handling of the very highest order that doesn't bite back. That car is the Porsche 944 Turbo the runt that became a prince.

FURTHER DEVELOPMENTS

Just two years after the Turbo's introduction, Porsche plugged the performance gap between the ordinary 944 and the Turbo with the 944S. Thanks to a cylinder head with four valves per cylinder and two overhead camshafts, this version developed 188bhp and had a top speed of over 140mph (225km/h) with 0–60mph (0–96km/h) acceleration in the 7-second bracket.

But this model did not have a long career. In 1989, the 944 range was rationalized down to two models – the Turbo (now with 250bhp) and the 944S2 powered by a 3-litre version of the 16-valve engine delivering an extremely healthy 211bhp and featuring not only a lighter cylinder block but, for the first time in any production car, a plastic oil sump. Cosmetically, the S2 assumed the 'Turbo look' and a very complete standard specification which included ABS brakes with ventilated discs all round and the wheels, tyres and suspension/damper settings of the original Turbo – a very necessary measure considering the S2's Turbo-aping performance: 146mph (235km/h) and 0–60mph (0–96km/h) in 6.0 secs, according to *Autocar & Motor*.

A year later a Cabriolet version was introduced which most observers thought was the prettiest 944 of all. It boasted an electrically operated hood yet, despite the powered head gear needed to achieve this, still retained useful plus 2 accommodation in the rear.

944 S (1987)

Engine

Longitudinal, front, rear-wheel drive

Capacity	2,479cc, 4-cyl in-line
Bore/Stroke	100/79mm
Compression ratio	10.9:1
Head/Block	Al alloy/Al alloy
Valve gear	Dohc, 4 valves per cylinder
Fuel and Ignition	Electronic ignition, Bosch Motronic fuel injection and engine management
Max Power	190bhp at 6,000rpm
Max Torque	144lb ft at 3,000rpm

Gearbox

Five-speed manual

Suspension

Front	Independent, single wishbones, MacPherson struts, coil springs, telescopic dampers, anti-roll bar
Rear	Independent, semi-trailing arms, transverse torsion bars, coil springs, telescopic dampers, anti-roll bar

Steering

Rack and pinion, power assistance

Brakes

Front	Ventilated discs
Rear	Ventilated discs
ABS	Optional

Wheels and Tyres

Cast alloy, 7×15in, 195/65 VR15 tyres

Dimensions

Length	165in (4,200mm)
Width	68.3in (1,735mm)
Height	50.2in (1,275mm)
Weight	2,822lb (1,280kg)

944 S2 (1987)

Engine

Longitudinal, front, rear-wheel drive

Capacity	2,990cc, 4-cyl in-line
Bore/Stroke	104/88mm
Compression ratio	10.9:1
Head/Block	Al alloy/Al alloy
Valve gear	Dohc, 4 valves per cylinder
Fuel and Ignition	Electronic ignition, Bosch Motronic fuel injection and engine management
Max Power	211bhp at 5,800rpm
Max Torque	207lb ft at 4,100rpm

Gearbox

Five-speed manual

Suspension

Front	Independent, single wishbones, MacPherson struts, coil springs, telescopic dampers, anti-roll bar
Rear	Independent, semi-trailing arms, transverse torsion bars, coil springs, telescopic dampers, anti-roll bar

Steering

Rack and pinion, power assistance

Brakes

Front	Ventilated discs
Rear	Ventilated discs
ABS	Standard

Wheels and Tyres

Cast alloy, 7×16in (front), 8×16in (rear), 205/55 VR16 (front), 225/50 VR16 (rear) tyres

Dimensions

Length	165in (4,200mm)
Width	68.3in (1,735mm)
Height	50.2in (1,275mm)
Weight	2,888lb (1,310kg)

944S2 versus principal rivals	BMW M3SE	M–B 190E 2.5–16 Evo	Porsche 944 S2	Audi Quattro 20V
Number of cylinders/valves	4/16	4/16	4/16	5/20
Displacement	2,467	2,498	2,990	2,226
Power output kW (bhp)	175 (238)	143 (195)	155 (211)	162 (221)
@ engine rpm	7,000	6,750	5,800	5,900
Maximum torque	240	235	280	309
(Nm) engine rpm	4,750	5,000	4,100	1,950
Output per litre kW/l	70.9	57.2	51.8	72.8
Compression ratio	10.2:1	9.7:1	10.9:1	9.3:1
Top speed mph (km/h)	154 (248)	143 (230)	149 (240)	143 (230)
Acceleration				
0–62mph (0–100km/h), secs	6.5	7.7	7.1	6.3
0–1,000m, secs	27.6	28.7	26.8	26.7
Unladen weight lb (kg)	2,640 (1,200)	2,860 (1,300)	2,948 (1,340)	3,036 (1,380)
Power/weight ratio kg/kW	6.9	9.1	8.6	8.5

Cutaway of 1986 944S: 16 valves, 190bhp and 142mph (228km/h).

4 968: The Story Continues

By the time the 924 was killed off in 1988, the 944 had already started to distance Porsche's good name and reputation from the down-market image and parts-bin engineering of what, in truth, had been a very pretty and effective sports coupé. But even the 944 was built for Porsche by Audi and, therefore, carried some of the old connotations. With the 80 per cent new 968 released in 1991, however, Zuffenhausen's sages believed that they had finally buried the 'pseudo Porsche' spectre of the 924 though, like the 944 it replaced, it was not truly a new car so much as another well-timed evolutionary spasm. The 968 tried hard in a number of ways, with radically new nose and tail treatment, a six-speed Getrag gearbox as standard, the option of Porsche's brilliant Tiptronic automatic transmission, variable valve timing for the 16-valve big-banger 'four' to give class-leading torque, an uprated chassis, bigger brakes, 911 Turbo style alloy wheels to cool them and a host of cosmetic niceties. Sharing the headlines was the far from inconsequential fact that it was built in Zuffenhausen by the same people who made 911s and 928s. Their experience, craftsmanship and attention to detail was now the 968's. Just as significant, however, was the dropping of the highly regarded Turbo model. According to Porsche's engineering boss, Paul Hensler, its development would have been prohibitively expensive, given, in the first place, the need to achieve at least 300bhp and then all the chassis and aerodynamic modifications that would go with it.

The 968's most important, and certainly most obvious, point of departure from the 944 was its styling which, as well as providing more progressive crumple characteristics in a crash, performed better in the wind tunnel, too, with a smaller frontal area factor and lower rear axle lift value, even if the Cd remained an unexceptional 0.34. A plainer interpretation of the changes, perhaps, was that the rounded nose with its exposed pop-up headlights and simpler tail made the 968 look as least as much like a 928 as the outgoing 944. Clearly, this played a big part in unifying the appearance of the front-engined range but crucially for the 968, it gave it the smell of a more expensive car.

ENGINE

The 3-litre, 16-valve four-cylinder engine that served the 944 S2 so well was still more potent in the 968. Peak power went up 14 per cent to 240bhp at 6,200rpm while maximum torque shot from an already impressive 207lb ft to 225lb ft at 4,100rpm, the highest output of any naturally aspirated 3-litre engine then in production. As before, the power plant featured twin contra-rotating balancer shafts to aid smoothness, Bosch Motronic injection and management and a closed loop, three-way exhaust catalytic converter with lambda regulation. Some of the extra power had been liberated by paying careful attention to intake manifold

Cutaway of 968 shows that while the body shape may have evolved, the basic architecture of the mechanicals hasn't. It also proves the original transaxle design had bags of potential. The 968 is good for over 150mph and 0–60mph in around 6 seconds.

and exhaust system design but the real star of the show was a variable valve timing system Porsche had patented as Variocam. This was a deceptively simple mechanism controlled by Motronic which, beyond 1,500rpm, acted on the camshaft chain tensioner to delay drive to the inlet camshaft by as much as 15 degrees. This gave progressive ignition advance at higher revs, hence the improved outputs. And the improved performance. Porsche claimed a top speed of 156mph (251km/h) and 0–60mph (0–96km/h) of 6.5secs for the six-speeder (not far off the old 944 Turbo's figures), 153mph (246km/h) and 7.9secs with Tiptronic.

GEARBOX

Made by Getrag, the six-speed gearbox was essentially the same as that used by Audi in its new S4 and had a double-H gate pattern with reverse on a dogleg out to the left. Maximum speed was achieved in sixth which meant that the intermediate ratios were very closely stacked. I asked Porsche's drivetrain chief, Paul Hensler, what was the point of developing an extra-torquey engine, only to give it the presumably unnecessary luxury of six speeds. 'It's simple,' he replied. 'Porsche drivers like changing gear.' Even, it would appear, if they drive an automatic.

968 (1991)

Engine

Longitudinal, front, rear-wheel drive

Capacity	2,990cc, 4-cyl in-line
Bore/Stroke	104/88mm
Compression ratio	11.0:1
Head/Block	Al alloy/Al alloy
Valve gear	Dohc, 4 valves per cylinder
Fuel and Ignition	Electronic ignition, Bosch Motronic multi-point fuel injection, three-way catalytic converter
Max Power	240bhp at 6,200rpm
Max Torque	225lb ft at 4,100rpm

Gearbox

Six-speed manual or four-speed Tiptronic

Suspension

Front	Independent, single wishbones, MacPherson struts, coil springs, telescopic dampers, anti-roll bar
Rear	Independent, semi-trailing arms, transverse torsion bars, coil springs, telescopic dampers, anti-roll bar

Steering

Rack and pinion, power assistance

Brakes

Front	Ventilated discs
Rear	Ventilated discs
ABS	Standard

Wheels and Tyres

Cast alloy, 7×16in (front), 8×16in (rear), Pirelli P700 Z tyres, 205/55 ZR16 (front), 225/50 ZR16 (rear)

Dimensions

Length	170in (4,320mm)
Width	68.3in (1,735mm)
Height	50.1in (1,275mm)
Weight	3,018lb (1,370kg)

Making Tiptronic an option was easy to understand. This dual-function automatic with its unique +/− manual shifting system and Intelligent Shift Programme that deliberately prevents upshifts before or in a corner worked superbly with the Carrera 2 and had been further refined for the 968. Hensler acknowledged its 'best of both

The 968's naturally aspirated 3-litre engine is the definitive expression of Porsche's balancer-shaft 'four' and employs 'Vari-Cam' variable valve timing. It is almost as powerful as the 944 Turbo's unit with 240bhp at 6,200rpm and 225lb ft of torque at 4,100rpm.

worlds' virtues but, personally, preferred the six-speeder. After his earlier comment, I somehow thought he would.

SUSPENSION

The 968 used the 944's suspension – wishbones, MacPherson struts and coils at the front, semi-trailing arms and transverse torsion bars at the rear, anti-roll bars at either end – but with spring and damper settings revised to give the 968 at least the tautness and control of the old 944 Turbo. 'Cup' design 16in cast alloy road wheels wearing 205/55 and 225/50 ZR rated tyres were standard but changed to 17in wheel of the same design fitted with 225/45 and 255/50 ZR tyres if the optional sports suspension was ordered with its adjustable dampers, height-adjustable spring platforms and still stiffer springs and dampers. The sports suspension pack also included larger front brakes, though, with ABS-backed ventilated discs and four-pot fixed callipers all round, the standard system was already formidable.

ON THE ROAD

And, in parts, so was the 968. I drove it for

The 968's designer, Harm Lagaay, described his handiwork as 'beautiful' at the time of its launch in 1992. Others weren't so sure, though many thought it striking and attractive. The front is smooth and integrated and has great presence but not so the back, which in the case of the Cabriolet looks as if it has an inverted tea-tray for a bootlid.

Autocar & Motor and found much to admire but also some surprising shortcomings:

> The power steering is meatily weighted yet so beautifully fluid and involving in its responses, you're seldom aware of it. And the cornering balance is lovely. The nose can be made to run wide if you're unrealistic about entry speeds, but mostly the 968 flows round bends with all four wheels sharing the workload – poised, unflappable, gripping tenaciously and indifferent to bumps yet eager to react to the driver's subtlest request. Easing the throttle draws the nose into the apex, a brush of brakes nudges the tail gently wide. Re-apply the power at this point and you can push it right out. And hold it. The 944 had one of the most rewarding rear-drive chassis in the business and the 968's is even better – crisper and quicker-reflexed but no harsher. The ride is firmer but not seriously so and its superior control is welcome on the autobahn.

> Fabulous brakes, great seats, solid build and virtually flawless paintwork and finish are all highlights of the 968's generally polished repertoire, too. But there are low spots which won't be easily ignored when the 968 goes on sale over here with an anticipated starting price of just over £40,000 for the manual coupé. Lusty and ultimately potent the new engine may be but, in its previous form, it never sounded this ragged, noisy and uncouth. Far from competing with the world's greatest six and eight cylinder engines, its lack of refinement and hammery raucousness at high revs is hard to believe for a four-cylinder engine and even harder to live with. A tingling vibration can be felt through all the pedals and the gear lever– not just at particular revs but at any revs.

> Neither does the Variocam 3-litre feel anything like as flexible as the torque graph might lead to expect – there's action aplenty above 3,000rpm, but not enough below it.

> In the light of this, the close ratio six-speed box begins to make some sense but, although good, its shift action isn't remotely slick enough to engender the 'let's change gear for the joy of it' reaction in drivers Paul Hensler claims to be its raison d'être. In the end, cog-swapping becomes a chore and it's easy to lose your way. A better bet is the Tiptronic but even this doesn't gel as well as it does with the 911, both seeming to sap an inordinate amount of acceleration and kicking down with an undignified thump. Somehow, though, it doesn't seem too bad having the steering wheel so close to your thighs when you only have to operate the brake pedal – while we're on the gripes, the driving position is no better than the 944's.

> All of which leaves me less sure about the 968 than I have been about any car for a long time. In an era when the competition grows stronger by the month and Porsche's reputation as a major force on the world's racing circuits is on the wane, it seems slightly perverse that the men from Zuffenhausen should entertain the extravagance of a 911 Turbo and not a parallel update of a much better road car, the 944 Turbo. As things stand, the 968 is too expensive and too uneven. A real Porsche it might be but that has to mean more than a brilliant chassis and a great body.

THE 968's RIVALS

Suspicions that the 968 was too little too late

hardened in the spring of 1992 when I flew to Detroit for a rendezvous with the 968 and two of its strongest rivals, the sensational new Mazda RX–7 and the dizzily high-tech Mitsubishi 3000 GT VR4. It was the first opportunity we'd had to test the Porsche's mettle and even as our KLM 747 touched down at motor city's Metro airport, no one was prepared to call the verdict . . .

The Porsche, an established superstar in this class as the 944 S2, has most to lose and what is almost certain to be the highest price to defend, at around £40,000. Whichever way you look at it, the 968 has its work cut out. Although its 3-litre engine is as big as the Mitsubishi's, it totes the least number of cylinders (four) and the fewest horses (240 at 6,200rpm) and not even one

turbocharger though, for many, the omission of a blower will be held up as an advantage. At 3,018lb, it's lighter than the technology-crammed 3,803lb, V6, 300bhp Mitsubishi but significantly heavier than the ultra-lean 2,800lb twin-rotor, 255bhp Mazda which walks away with the power/weight ratio prize, laying down a figure of 201bhp/tonne to the Porsche's 175bhp/tonne and the Mitsubishi's 174bhp/tonne. Anticipated prices for the 3000 GT VR4 and RX–7 are £35,000 and £25,000 respectively so the Mazda is odds on to win the performance-per-£ contest by a country mile (this turned out not to be the case, UK RX–7s coming loaded with equipment and a price tag £10,000 higher than expected). Brute force isn't every

The 968's slant-four 3–litre engine featured VariCam, Porsche's patented mechanical variable valve timing.

968 Club Sport (1992)

Engine

Longitudinal, front, rear-wheel drive

Capacity	2,990cc, 4-cyl in-line
Bore/Stroke	104/88mm
Compression ratio	11.0:1
Head/Block	Al alloy/Al alloy
Valve gear	Dohc, 4 valves per cylinder
Fuel and Ignition	Electronic ignition, Bosch Motronic DME multi-point fuel injection, three-way catalytic converter
Max Power	240bhp at 6,200rpm
Max Torque	225lb ft at 4,100rpm

Gearbox

Six-speed manual

Suspension

Front	Independent, single wishbones, MacPherson struts, coil springs, telescopic dampers, anti-roll bar
Rear	Independent, semi-trailing arms, transverse torsion bars, coil springs, telescopic dampers, anti-roll bar

Steering

Rack and pinion, power assistance

Brakes

Front	Ventilated discs
Rear	Ventilated discs
ABS	Standard

Wheels and Tyres

Cast alloy, 7.5×17in (front), 9×17in (rear), Yokohama A008, 225/45 ZR17 (front), 255/40 ZR17 (rear)

Dimensions

Length	170in (4,320mm)
Width	68.3in (1,735mm)
Height	50.1in (1,275mm)
Weight	2,937lb (1,335kg)

thing, of course. The Porsche hits back with a six-speed gearbox (five-speeders for the other two), an ingenious variable valve timing system, one of the world's great rear-drive chassis, a beautifully-trimmed two-plus-two cabin and a peerless reputation for build quality. Also it's a Porsche and all that stands for, a factor which shouldn't be underestimated.

The RX–7's ace card used to be the fact that it had a Wankel engine but that's no longer enough. Now that engine, the 1,308cc twin-rotor 13B receives the attentions of the most sophisticated turbocharging systems since the Porsche 959's. Its intercooler-fed, sequential twin turbos seek to deliver power and torque across a broader rev range than conventional turbos with minimal lag: 255bhp and 217lb ft of torque say Mazda got its figures right. And to make the most of the outputs, the new RX–7 is *very* light – not, it should be noted, through the use of exotic materials, but ruthless implementation of fat-paring detail, the time-honoured but still remarkably effective a-few-pounds-here-a-few-pounds-there method. Not only is the body lighter but stiffer (by 20 per cent) and sleeker, with the Cd dropping to 0.29.

It's also the benefactor of an all-new suspension system with wishbones all round replacing the previous struts and trailing arms and a sophisticated Torsen limited slip differential to help the rear end get a grip in slippery conditions. The brakes are colossal for a car so light (11.6in vented discs front and rear) and get 225/50 VR 16 tyres on 8in alloy rims to work with.

The stunningly-styled Mitsubishi 3000 GT VR4 could hardly be more diverse in its design philosophy. It's an all singing, all dancing technology showcase. Four-wheel drive, four-wheel steering, microprocessor-controlled damping, twin turbochargers, automatically activated spoilers – they all have a place on the quad-cam, 24-valve, 3-litre, 300bhp V6.

Mazda RX–7

Initially the Mazda doesn't seem all that quick. A slow, exploratory depression of the accelerator pedal produces an equally unhurried, if stupendously smooth, stroll into the middle regions of the rotary engine's remarkably broad rev range. You wouldn't feel inclined to call this part-throttle activity snappy. Indeed, if you back off, the strong flywheel effect of the rotors seems to delay the message and then exacerbate some slackness in the driveline. As a result of this, the RX–7 isn't the easiest of cars to drive smoothly in traffic. Set your ankle at a sharper angle, though, and any suggestions of lethargy are swept aside by the sheer eagerness of the suddenly galvanized twin-turbo Wankel motor to hurl the rev counter needle towards 8,000rpm and bounce the back of your head against the seat. The big push starts at around 2,500rpm as the first turbo – designed to do its best work at low to medium revs – hits peak form. Before the power curve has a chance to tail off, however, the second turbo, already up to speed, grabs the initiative and runs. Make intelligent use of the stubby gearlever with its quick, short-throw action and well-judged ratios, and the Mazda's ground-covering ability is nothing short of breathtaking.

According to Mazda, the relay tactics of the turbos should ensure a seamless flow of power but, in practice, there's no mistaking the moment the second turbo's contribution starts. It's like a jet kicking in the afterburners and never fails to thrill. Ambitious as Mazda's 158mph and 4.9secs 0–60mph claims look on paper, we wouldn't bet against them: on our 60-mile road circuit striking out from Ann Arbor, the Mazda always held a comfortable margin over the Porsche and the Mitsubishi when it came to overtaking other traffic. Even so, the rotary powerplant has its drawbacks. It may be as smooth as a turbine but it sounds like one, too, its most purposeful note being a muted anodyne hum which, while unobtrusive, is unlikely to stimulate those who expect a well-tuned sonic performance from their sportscars to anything like the same degree as the Mitsubishi's deepchested howl or the 968's cultured rasp. And as well as the part-throttle shortcomings already noted, the elimination of turbo lag isn't quite as complete as Mazda would have you believe. Punch open the throttle and, just occasionally, there's a moment of conspicuous calm before the storm.

Mitsubishi 3000 GT VR4

Contrastingly, the Mitsubishi's twinturbos blow simultaneously and don't appear to have any lag worth mentioning. Part-throttle performance is undoubtedly more progressive and consistent than the Mazda's and, at anything up to two-thirds throttle opening, the GT's power delivery feels comparatively effortless and buoyant. But while the Mitsubishi's generous stash of turbo-enhanced torque moves it along at an impressive lick, there isn't much left in the bank when you want to make a serious withdrawal. On our Michigan-registered example, at any rate, it felt as if the management system was holding its quad-cam V6 charge in check – not allowing it full expression with the right-hand pedal clamped to the metal. A GT previously tried in Britain packed the sort of top end elan you expect from 300bhp and concomitant with the 150mph and

5.6secs 0–60mph performance claims. Even so, our Mitsubishi hit hard enough to hold its own in give and take conditions, had the most sporting engine note (subtly amplified when you flick a switch identified by an exhaust silencer graphic to 'sport' mode) and felt the most relaxed cruiser. It had the worst – or perhaps we should say least slick – gearchange with a slightly 'detached' feeling shift that also displays some across-gate notchiness. The GT's clutch is surprisingly light, though, and the ratios well-spaced, if somewhat long.

Porsche 968

Let's bring the 968 into this argument. Even the Mitsubishi's alert responses to the throttle are made to seem torpid by the immediacy and linearity of the 968's. Also terrific is the breadth of the big four's power band. Only at low revs in sixth gear does it feel lame. Most of the time the 16-valver pulls with genuinely deep-chested flexibility and has the most usable mid-range urge of the group. The so-called Variocam valve timing system can delay drive to the inlet camshaft by up to 15 degrees and this gives progressive ignition advance at higher revs, hence the improved outputs.

Like the 3000 GT, however, it doesn't come close to matching the white hot pick up of the RX–7 at high revs. Nor does it rev as high (red line at 6,500rpm) or with the same uncanny smoothness, though with the help of its twin contra-rotating balancer shafts, it does all right for a 'big banger' four. The engine is flexible enough for Porsche to look on the sixth speed as an economy overdrive rather than a device for squashing up the other ratios

*The pop-up lamp frontal treatment of the 968 caused some controversy but was, in fact,
the blueprint for a new Porsche family look as confirmed by the appearance of the new 911
in 1993.*

*The 968 Cabrio went on sale in the spring of 1992 and immediately proved popular,
taking over where the 944 S2 left off.*

but, even so, there are no holes in the power delivery. One of the great joys of driving the 968 is giving the engine its head through the gears: savouring the hard, crisp punch between 3,000 and 5,000rpm as each new gear snaps into the heart of the torque band, finding tactile reward from the slick precision of the close-gate gearchange. The beautifully measured urgency of it all is a potent experience, even if the factory figures of 156mph and 0–60mph in 6.5secs trail those of its Japanese rivals.

Ride and Handling

Straight line speed alone, however, was never going to be conclusive on twisting roads crumbled and pocked marked by Michigan's large seasonal and night/day temperature extremes. Here each car provides viable solutions but, again, one car stands out. Despite the past glories of the 944, it isn't the 968. In isolation, it's hard to pick fault with the Porsche's chassis. The Zuffenhausen engineers have a certain way of doing things that's instantly recognizable in the newcomer: steering that, while not especially direct, is nicely damped, creamily consistent and decently informative; turn in that avoids twitchiness but isn't devoid of bite; a proper role for the throttle in determining cornering attitude and, of course, that wonderful sense of balance that allows the driver a full range of options between mild understeer and easily controllable oversteer. Add to that strong grip and suspension supple enough to take the sting out of the pitted and scarred bitumen and you have bones of a great chassis.

In the context of the other two, though, its limitations (and we never thought we'd be using that word) become obvious. For all its excessive weight and bulk, the Mitsubishi comfortably out-corners the Porsche. True, it doesn't have the feel and balance of the German car – it isn't the *personal* tool – but neither are its responses quite as aloof or artificial as you'd imagine. If the object is simply to get round the twists with the maximum of speed and security and the minimum of fuss and drama, the all-drive VR4 is a formidable piece of machinery. Turn in is slightly sharper than the Porsche's and its steering, while short of useful feedback, feels more direct. Power can be fed in surprisingly early without understeer becoming a problem. The pay-off, here, is storming exit speed; the Mitsubishi bursts out of bends like a cork from a champagne bottle.

As with other ESC-equipped Mitsubishis, the best handling/comfort compromise is to be found in 'normal' mode. The 'sport' setting makes the ride harder without seeming to confer any significant advantage on the handling. It's an important point since combining good ride comfort with fine suspension control is the GT's strong suit.

A cossetting ride wasn't the first thing on the minds of Mazda's managers when they sent their top engineers kart racing to fine tune the seats of their pants prior to starting work on the RX–7. Their aim was to build a sports car with uncompromised, undiluted handling excellence, a car that would set a world standard in this discipline. The performance-orientated 'R1' pack fitted to our Californian-registered test car takes this philosophy as far as it can go with firmer spring and damper settings, spoilers front and rear and Z-rated tyres.

The result is a revelation. Here is a

car which makes the 968 feel soft, woolly and imprecise, a car with more outright grip than the four-wheel drive Mitsubishi. A car all about response, grip and finesse. Imagine an MX–5, with all of its immediacy, intimacy and incisiveness intact, but blessed with the grip of an industrial strength electro-magnet, the suspension control of a Formula One car and the balance of a prima ballerina. That's how it seems behind the wheel of the Mazda. With just 2.9 turns between locks, the steering is very direct geared but, on the move, it feels even swifter and more precise than the figure suggests. Feedback isn't quite as well resolved as the Porsche's but turn in is simply fabulous – on an altogether higher plateau. In tight bends, the rotary engine's ample torque can be used to break traction at the back but so progressive is the breach and so quick-witted the steering's responses that correction is as natural as breathing.

The ride is very firm but not harsh. The very fact that it coped with the worst Detroit could throw at it is testament to its bottom line acceptability. You ride over the bumps and thump into the dips but so stiff is the body shell and so well damped the suspension that it's far from being a filling-loosening experience.

Braking is exemplary on all three, the Porsche winning for pedal feel, the RX–7 for ultimate stopping power. The Mitsubishi's only real problem is a slightly over-servoed pedal action – it hauls off speed rapidly and, in common with the others, resists fade.

Driver Comfort

The Mazda's driving environment mirrors the single-mindedness of its road behaviour. Its chunky, three-spoke steering wheel is a little larger than expected but allows clear sight of all the instruments through the upper portion. A big rev counter occupies centre stage with a slightly smaller speedo to the right and the minor gauges grouped to the left. The nostalgically chromed bezels don't really work in the context of the otherwise ultra-modern facia but the classically marked dials look good and are easy to read.

Despite the lack of any height or tilt adjustment for the cushion, there's ample rearward travel for tall drivers and the well-planned major control relationships – not least the heel and toe orientated spacing of the (drilled metal) brake and accelerator pedals – contribute to an excellent driving position. The shapely seats have plenty of under thigh and lateral support and good padding for the small of the back. Although the cabin is quite narrow, the doors have scooped out panels to liberate a little more elbow room: even so, the abiding impression is of a cosy, efficient interior that wraps round the driver. The space where Mazda might have been tempted to put a couple of 'plus 2' seats has, more sensibly, been used to house two deep, lockable cubbies.

More expansive in every way is the Mitsubishi's cabin. It sets out to look complex and succeeds. The switchgear is conspicuous in its generosity, less so its specificity. Some of the switches aren't easy to find, some clearly afterthoughts. This isn't to detract from the general design of the facia which, while American in style with contoured cowels for the auxiliary gauges, makes good provision for the major instruments which are large, neat and clear. The steering wheel boss is big enough to accommodate a row of duplicate controls for the stereo and the wheel itself adjusts for rake angle.

Electric motors move the GT's cushion for reach, tilt and height and the backrest's lateral wings and lumbar support but the backrest rake is manual. After a little experimentation, it's possible to tailor a near-ideal driving position but, despite its plethora of adjustment possibilities, the seat itself doesn't quite live up to its promise. The token rear seats aren't meant for adults and, presumably, would be a squeeze for small children.

And the same level of token rear seat accommodation exists in the more familiar Porsche cabin. The 968's front seats, however, are even better than the Mazda's and its pedals best of all for heel and toe downshifts. Still afflicted slightly by the wheel-in-lap syndrome, the Porsche's driving position is nevertheless very comfortable and complemented by clear, comprehensive instrumentation and good all round visibility – marginally the best of the three.

Conclusion

When it comes to the final reckoning, though, the Porsche doesn't assume its customary ascendancy this time round. You can make a strong case for the flexibility and responsiveness of its engine, the poise and balance of its chassis, the excellence of its build quality and the sheer feeling of finely honed engineering the car exudes at all times. Taken together, these virtues are enough to keep the 968's nose in front of the Mitsubishi which, for all its shining technology and undeniable ability, offers a rather detached driving experience and is simply too big and heavy to feel truly agile and involving.

In the end, it's the RX–7 that steals victory. It isn't quite as well rounded and cohesive as the Porsche, nor as overtly high-tech as the Mitsubishi. Question marks hang over its part throttle response and ride comfort and there's no space for kids in the back. On the other hand, it's probably the most focused sports car we've ever driven, a car dedicated to pure, unadulterated driving pleasure. It looks sexy, goes like a jet and handles like a dream. Even if it wasn't the cheapest it would win. As it is, we wonder if there's been a contest.

GOODWOOD TRIAL

The 968 had a chance to get its own back later on that year when seven of the world's best-handling cars, as selected by *Autocar & Motor*, were required to lock horns at the formidably fast and demanding Goodwood circuit. Both the 968 and its precociously gifted Japanese rival were present to represent the front-engined, rear-driven way of doing things and, in the end, both had to concede defeat to Honda's phenomenal NSX. Even so, the Porsche ran the RX–7 a lot closer than many imagined it would:

> The inevitable clash between the 968 and the RX–7 turned out to be every bit as violent as expected and more controversial than anyone could have guessed. Of the two, it was the Porsche that polarized opinion more sharply. The pro-camp pointed to the feel and balance of the 968, the uncanny way it resolved road information at the helm and the alacrity with which the cornering line could be adjusted by the throttle.
>
> Andrew Frankel spoke for many: 'Deceptively fast, endlessly forgiving (almost) and so, so friendly. Best

steering by far of the powered set-ups; lovely, chunky wheel. Understeer could become pronounced, especially in Lavant corner, but you could so easily dial it all out with the merest relaxation of your right foot, it never bothered me. Indeed, if you turned in on a trailing throttle and then went back on the power, it would go all beautifully neutral and drift round all of a piece.'

This, however, wasn't Sutcliffe's experience. 'It scared me on two or three occasions,' he admitted, 'and as far as I'm concerned I hadn't done a whole lot wrong to deserve it. Just the slightest hint of backing off the throttle going into St Mary's meant great armfuls of opposite lock. And once, going through Fordwater, all I did was miss the apex by a foot or three and I thought I was destined for Basingstoke, via the nearest field.'

Or mine. I was one of the three people to spin the Porsche during the day. It didn't have the turn-in bite, suspension control or the iron stability of the Mazda. Everything else stayed on the track. Interestingly, the 968 was also far harder on its tyres than the Mazda, eventually chewing off lumps of tread. At close of play, the RX–7's tyres looked virtually unused. The arguments raged on, though. 'Superb response from the chassis,' said Lyon. 'Not a car to take liberties with,' countered Thomas. 'Responsive and poised,' asserted Production Editor Mark Harrop. 'Simply not as good as the Mazda,' concluded European Editor Peter Robinson.

5 On the Track

RACING THE 924

Although the notion that the 924 would participate in motorsport seems an obvious one now – both from the platform of precedent (the Zuffenhausen marque and racing were inseparable) and the need to pump a little macho glamour into the front-engined coupé's rather pedestrian portfolio – it was the last thing on Porsche's corporate mind when the car was launched in 1976. In the event, its competition career spanned four years, from 1978 to 1982, and garnered a respectable collection of silverware considering that its track prowess was never taken all that seriously by the factory.

The idea that a 924 might be able to cut it in competition was, in part, floated by Porsche GB but since there were no races for which the car had been homologated, its track début came by way of a one-make challenge on British circuits. The brainchild of managing director John Aldington and organized by the British Automobile Racing Club, the one-make series had the desired effect, putting a spring into the step of the 924's 1978 sales graph. Not so in America, where the base model's progress seemed to be all backwards: 13,696 sales for the year of launch, 1977, falling back to 8,387 in 1979. An expedient excuse was to blame the weak dollar but Porsche knew as well as anyone that the problem lay with the car's image – or rather, the fact that, in the public's eyes at least, it didn't seem to have one.

The first meeting of the '924 Championship' was held at Donington in April 1978. Far from being an 'out-of-the-box' racer, the 924 was let down by its rear drum brakes which, while fine for road use, were asked to work too hard by the combination of grippy slick racing tyres made specially for the car by Dunlop and the extra 20 per cent of power liberated by blueprinting the engines. The good drivers knew how to compensate for this, none better than journalist-racer Tony Dron who won the inaugural Championship driving an entry sponsored by dairy owner Geoff Fox. In doing so, he resisted the challenge of talented and experienced full-time tin top campaigners such as Andy Rouse, Chris Craft and Barrie 'Whizzo' Williams.

But despite the closeness of the racing, obvious spectator approval and the beneficial effect it was having on 924 sales, there wasn't a Championship in 1979. Ironically, the dealers – whose support the series needed for its survival – found themselves too busy selling cars to prepare them for racing. Although a couple of dealers (notably AFN and Gordon Lamb) kept their cars going and managed to lift a handful of endurance records, that was basically that.

Despite the odd private endeavour (the most notable being that of Porsche's customer relations manager Jurgen Barth who finished a very creditable 20th in the 1979 Monte Carlo Rally with a pre-Turbo homologation, 125bhp) the next chapter in the 924's competition career was written in the United States.

The same problem (limp-wristed image) was met with a more daring solution. The grid line-ups for the October 1979 SCCA National series run-offs would be sprinkled with 924 D-Production models, a special 924 designed at Weissach and built in limited

Gerry Marshall about to blast off in the Lamb 924. From left to right, Roy Pierpoint, Jack Sears, Barrie 'Whizzo' Williams and Tony Lanfranci look on.

numbers at Warrington, Pennsylvania by Al (son of Porsche dealer and one-time racer Bob) Holbert.

Thanks to a hike in capacity from 1,984 to 2,037cc, a high compression ratio (11.9:1) and the replacement of the Bosch K-Jetronic fuel injection with the Bosch-Kugelfischer system, power leapt from 125 to 185bhp, developed now at a heady 7,500rpm. Dry sump lubrication, the Turbo model's chassis (vented discs at the rear, five-stud wheel fixings, Bilstein gas-filled dampers), the adoption of 15×7in BBS alloy rims and the replacement of door and hatch glass with Plexiglass to reduce weight to 970kg added further ammunition to the starter Porsche's track credibility.

The DP's first outing, at Atlanta in October 1979, didn't. Neither of the two cars entered finished in the top ten but then, at this early stage, chassis development was far from complete. By the following winter, with the spring rates softened up considerably, the eight competing DPs found winning ways, the 1980 series finally falling to 'Doc' Bundy in a Holbert Racing-entered car. The following year the 924 received a showroom boost in the shape of the 924 but in the SCCA finals at Road Atlanta Bundy's thunder was stolen by arch rival Tom Brennan, both driving normally aspirated 924s, when the heavens opened and the 'Doc's' wipers froze on the screen.

Impressive and entertaining road car as it turned out to be, the 924 Turbo seemed to fire the factory with little more enthusiasm

The 1979 Gordon Lamb 924 proves that you don't need wide tyres and flared arches to go racing.

for competition than had the 'cooking' 924. The Carrera GT, though, was a different matter. Unveiled at the Frankfurt Show in September 1979, it boasted an out-of-the-box 210bhp from its 1,984cc, turbocharged and intercooled engine and used flared polyurethane wheelarches to cover the new 7J×15in (16in optional) forged alloy wheels. The 400-off homologation production run was quickly snapped up by enthusiasts and Weissach's engineering department wasted no time in turning the Carrera GT into a serious race car that could and would compete at Le Mans.

The process saw the Carrera stiffened, lightened and kept respectably aerodynamic (a Cd of 0.35 against the regular Carrera GT's 0.34 despite 11 and 12in rims front and rear). Titanium springs (coils at the back supplementing the standard torsion bars) and gas-filled Bilstein dampers helped make the most of the chassis, as did the 100 per cent limited slip differential. More dramatic changes were deemed unnecessary since the increases in power and torque were

relatively modest: peak bhp went from 210 to 320, maximum torque from 202 to 282lb ft. The extra muscle had been achieved by running a larger intercooler and higher boost pressure and replacing the usual Bosch K-Jetronic fuel injection with a Bosch/Kugelfischer mechanical system.

But despite the reduction in weight from 1,180 to just 930kg, the racing Carrera GT (or type 937 as it was called), proved only just fast enough to qualify for Le Mans, managing a comparatively pedestrian 175mph (281km/h) down the Mulsanne straight. For once, Porsche knew it wouldn't win the race but might triumph against an indifferent public in giving the 924's somewhat lacklustre image an invaluable shine and paving the way for the forthcoming 944 model.

In the event, the three works 924s did better than anyone had dared hope. Driving responsibilities fell to British, German and American teams: Tony Dron and Andy Rouse, Jurgen Barth and Manfred Schurti, and Derek Bell and Al Holbert respectively.

The un-liveried 924 Carrera GT for Le Mans in 1980. Its 1,984cc engine developed 320bhp at 6,500rpm.

The race started wet – good news for the underpowered Carreras which made up what they lacked in grunt and straightline speed in agility and their ability to slice through the standing water. Bell did best in the early laps, posting a 16th overall after the first hour, with Barth and Rouse back in a more expected 22nd and 28th places.

By breakfast on Sunday, however, the positions had improved to a 6–7–8 run, but not for long. Misfires started to plague two of the cars, eventually knocking several cylinders out of action with an overlean mixture dictated by the increasingly shaky mechanical injection – not exactly a luxury when you start out with four. The answer was to enrich the fuel mixture, a measure which enabled the Barth/Schurti car to continue at undiminished pace and finish an outstanding 6th. One cylinder down, the Bell/Holbert partnership did well to hang on to 13th

while Rouse and Dron – a mere brace of pots still hanging in – barely made it across the finishing line to take 12th place.

THE 924 GTP

That unprecedented 6th place was undoubtedly the apogee of the 924's racing career. The so-called 924GTP ('P' for prototype) which competed at Le Mans in 1981 was, in fact, a racing testbed for the forthcoming 944 model. But despite its uprated engine, 11th was the best the GTP (driven by Manfred Schurti and Andy Rouse) could do.

The key to the GTP's potential, of course, was its all-new, all-aluminium 2,479cc engine. Its extra capacity came from the big 100mm bore, the stroke remaining comparatively short, at 78.9mm. With a 16-valve

Number 2 is Derek Bell's 924 Carrera GT which was part of a team of three 924s entered at Le Mans in 1980.

head and exhaust-driven KKK turbocharger it developed, without much strain, a reliable 420bhp. Clearly evident in this early competition version were the twin contra-rotating balancer shafts that would later be credited with making the 944's engine so smooth for a 'big banger' four. Another 944 feature, but almost unheard of at Le Mans, was the Bosch Motronic injection/engine management which used microprocessors for ignition mapping, fuel flow, boost pressure and knock sensing – a far cry from the mechanical injection systems of the previous year.

You wouldn't necessarily have suspected the extra sophistication looking at the new Carrera GTP. There were thicker brake discs and various weight saving measures

that shaved the weight to 950kg when it was scrutineered at the Norisring two weeks after Le Mans. But the chassis was essentially unchanged from the year before; likewise the Boss sponsorship livery. Drivers were Jurgen Barth and Walter Rohrl.

A one-off engine design rather than a precursor to the 16-valve unit that would later power the 944S, it had crossflow cooling instead of Porsche's more usual longitudinal arrangement, and single belt cam drive rather than the combination of belts and chains for the production 16-valve heads.

With the turbo wound up to 1.5bar, the engine was capable of delivering 500bhp but raced with 1.1bar boost and 420bhp – a good blend of brawn and reliability. In its début

The 1982 Canon-Porsche 924 Carrera GTR turbo which finished fifth overall in the Nurburgring 1000kms on 30 May.

Richard Lloyd (now proprietor of VW tuners GTi Engineering) testing his 924 GTR.

race at Le Mans 1982 driven by Barth and Rohrl, it finished a creditable 7th overall.

RACING THE 944

The 924 GTP's career ended with the arrival of the 944 Turbo which spawned its own one-make series in 1985, both in Europe and America. In America, the Turbo also raced against (and usually beat) Chevrolet Corvettes, Camaros, Saab Turbos, Maserati Biturbos and Mazda RX–7s.

The Americans took to the 944 as a competition car and ran it in both the SCCA and IMSA categories. The 944 Turbo made its racing début in the Nelson Ledges 24-hour event in Ohio in July 1984. The entry would be driven by Jim Busby, Rick Knoop and Porsche dealer Freddy Baker, competing against fifty-five other 'production cars', all gleaming and with emission-free exhaust systems and showroom tyres. B. F. Goodrich provided the latter free of charge.

Pole position placed the Porsche ahead of Chevrolet Corvettes, Camaros and many other European hopefuls, even including a few Maserati Biturbos. It didn't matter, the 944 Turbo simply walked away from the field, finishing with a forty-two lap advantage over the second place car, a normally aspirated 944 driven by Rick and Jamie Hurst and BFG engineer Bob Strange. Regular 944s also took fourth and fifth.

Al Holbert, motorsport boss of Porsche Cars North America (a wholly factory-owned subsidiary) spearheaded Porsche's efforts to make a mark in SCCA and IMSA GTO/GTU categories. Looking for an edge, he returned to the spaceframe chassis of his previously successful 924 racer. A similar spaceframe was built to accommodate a modified (525bhp – some modification!) 944 Turbo engine. The car appeared as the 944 GTR at the SCCA's Road Atlanta run-offs in October 1985. It wasn't on the pace, a matter

944s have always been cars you can race virtually 'straight out of the box'.

former Porsche employee Alwin Springer sought to rectify in the winter. He felt that the engine was built for strength and longevity rather than explosive power. He appreciated the former but wanted more of the latter.

His development work was so extensive that the 2.5-litre turbo, 600bhp-plus engine he ended up with bore little resemblance to the one he started with. This one couldn't fail. But it did. Financial problems, in-house wrangling and constant rule changing by the SCCA saw to that. The Ludwig Heimrath father and son team gave the GTR its only races in 1986, but with limited success.

Still, there was always next year. And initially things started to look up. New Zealander Bruce Jenner formed a two-car team with Elliot Forbes-Robinson and secured backing from Olivetti. Sure enough, EFR won at Brainerd but, following that, the SCCA regulations changed once again and the car lost its competitive edge.

111

944 and 911 battle it out on the track. Although technically the more conventional and 'workable' racer with its front engine/transaxle layout and near 50:50 weight distribution, the 944 has always played second fiddle to the phenomenally successful rear-engined old-timer.

That was effectively curtains for the GTR. It had already been sidelined by the Indycar project and when Al Holbert died at the controls of his light aircraft late in 1988, the GTR died with him. From now on, the 944 Turbo would compete only in one-make series.

The Porsche Turbo Cup series was announced in 1985 – seven races on German circuits, each with prize money totalling DM45,000. Within reason, the cars would run in standard trim, the engines nominally rated at 220bhp running on lead-free fuel and with catalytic converters in place. Turbo Cup cars were offered at a special price of DM78,900 to genuine racing customers and forty were made for delivery in March 1986.

Roland Asch dominated the series over its four seasons. The winner of the first series, however, was the late Manfred Winkelhock's talented young brother, Joachim. In 1987, the Turbo Cup spread its net outside Germany with extra races being held at

Brno (Czechoslovakia), the Salzburgring (Austria), Spa (Belgium), Jarama (Spain) and Monza (Italy). Ten rounds made up the series. Another forty cars were built with the production car's up-rated 250bhp engine, ABS anti-lock brakes and numerous suspension improvements. The price of the cars leapt up to DM95,000 but the increased prize money (up to DM54,000 per event) went some way to offsetting this.

The cars had put on a little weight but still provided very exciting racing. They were quick, too: 0–62mph (0–100km/h) in 5.7secs, 0–100mph (0–160km/h) in 14.5secs, a standing kilometre time of 24.5secs and a top speed of over 160mph (257km/h).

Asch's domination of the series reached its apogee in the 1989 season driving for the Paul-Ernst Straehle team. His reward? To be given a Mercedes works-backed drive in the 1990 German Touring Car championship for Alain Cudini's team. Rich irony indeed.

6 Riding the Storm

'The next two years will be very difficult,' said Arno Bohn, then chairman of Porsche, in 1992. He was right in more ways than he could have known. Early the following year he was to lose his job to Wendelin Weidking. Porsche's predicament, however, would not go away. In the US, sales had fallen below the 5,000 mark. In Japan and the UK they were about to reach rock bottom. And to make matters worse, the domestic market had also started to decline. But the clouds of doom had gathered before over Zuffenhausen. Both Bohn and his successor believed that Porsche was tough enough to weather the storm; that having an attractive model range was crucial to Porsche's plight and pointed to the 928 GTS and the new 968 as the models that would pull the company through. But thus far, customer reaction to the updated four-cylinder model had been lukewarm. In Germany, the 968 had in three months collected only 500 orders, and even in the States, where it sold for an aggressive $39,950 (£21,600), the queues were not as long as Porsche had hoped. The profit margin on the US model was wafer-thin. But there was no option but to price the car close to chief rivals such as the Nissan 300ZX and Lexus SC400. The plan was to increase production to 130 units a day, the highest rate ever. The output of the new 928 GTS was scheduled to increase from one to ten cars, the 968 to thirty, and the 911 to sixty-eight units. The remaining twenty-two vehicles were 500Es built for Mercedes.

The figures looked promising, but, if realized, Porsche's total output would go up only because all models were now being built at the Porsche plant in Zuffenhausen and not by Audi, who used to make the 944 at Neckarsulm. In fact, the number of Porsches built would actually fall, and the 1992 forecast called for a further drop in production to around 23,000 units. There would also be a sharp decline in earnings from around £13 million to £3 million.

RUMOURS OF A SALE

Although Porsche has repeatedly denied that it is up for sale, the rumours persist. Reliable sources say Ferry Porsche and his sister Louise Piech do not want to sell, but others might accept the right offer. At this point, even the conservative family members are beginning to worry, because it is transparently clear that the £200 million the company has in the bank will not cover the investment programme for the next five years. It must either accept the risk and borrow money from the bank or sell up while the bidders are still keen to write fat cheques.

Among the most ardent speculators are Mercedes-Benz, VW/Audi and BMW. But there is also an all-German solution on the cards which would give Mercedes, VW and BMW an equal share – possibly favourite now that Mercedes is facing its own financial crisis. This proposal is an interesting one for Weissach, which could become a collective think-tank for the German motor industry. At this point, however, none of these proposals has been given the green light. Instead, the Porsche and Piech families are discussing the possibility of an increase in capital which would speed up cashflow without affecting the company's treasured independence.

And if all this has a ring of familiarity, it should come as no surprise. Porsche has always been vulnerable to fluctuating exchange rates and the fickle nature of the North American market. In November 1983, Ernst Piech, one of Dr Porsche's Austrian hotel-owning nephews, told the family that he wished to sell his 9.5 per cent shareholding, valued at DM100million, to Kuwaiti-owned Al-Mal and Saudi-owned ABS Daus banks. An urgent meeting of the family planned the next move and decided to take up his holding. It seemed that disaster had been averted by the slimmest of margins. But within weeks it became clear that Dr Porsche's sister, Louise Piech, had been wooed by the same deal and announced her intention to sell out to the consortium. The remaining eight family members found that they could not cover this second move – pure soap opera.

Only one course of action was feasible. On 17 April, 1984, a block of non-voting shares in Dr Ing hc F. Porsche AG was placed on the Stuttgart, Frankfurt and Munich stock exchanges. This action alone raised the nominal capital value of the company from DM50 million to DM70 million, of which half was offered to the public. The shares were snapped up rapidly, the value of each nominal DM50 share initially rising to DM110. Literally overnight Porsche had 35,000 shareholders instead of ten, but the helm of the company remained securely in the family's hands and disaster was averted.

Porsche has always understood the inevitability of being backed up between a rock and a hard place from time to time, and the best ways to avoid being crushed. The circumstances surrounding the launch of the Carrera 4 are a case in point. It went on sale in the autumn of 1988 and clearly, against a background of falling profits, it was not a moment too soon. Clearly, the 911 would only survive and prosper if Porsche did the same and the company's performance for 1988 gave little cause for optimism at Zuffenhausen.

At the root of Porsche's problems, as before, was an over-reliance on the American market at the time of a falling dollar exchange rate. The situation was not helped by what was already being recognized as the burden of sustaining three model ranges – 944, 928 and 911. 'It must be our aim to plan for a future in which we shall use two basic types to concentrate entirely on the exclusive and expensive end of the market', said Ferry Porsche. The catalyst for this new thrust came in the 1987/88 business year when the share of vehicles exported to the United States dropped from 65 to less than 40 per cent, and in the first six months of 1989, sales fell from 8,806 to 4,556 units. The news was bad enough for newly appointed chairman Heinz Branitzky to concede: 'This is undoubtedly the most difficult year we have ever had in America'. However, he did add: 'The worst is behind us'.

RELYING ON THE 911

Porsche's chronic problem had been an over-reliance on the 911 model, then ten years old and made at a rate of 15–16,000 a year in good times. Back in 1974 demand slumped dangerously, only 11,800 being built in that model year and financially Porsche only broke even. Things went from bad to worse in 1975 with production dipping below 9,000 cars, of which the Americans bought an inconsequential 4,732. By this time, the 911 Turbo was on the starting blocks and destined for great things commercially, but it couldn't cure Porsche's malaise all by itself. The 911 Turbo, was perhaps, the star pupil of Dr Fuhrmann's nine-year reign. After all, it was on his insistence that the 400 examples needed for Group 4 homologation in 1976 were comprehensively equipped and luxurious flagships. The clear-sightedness of this decision was only fully appreciated when the Turbo became a cult-status supercar, with sales averaging between 1,000 and 2,000 a year.

Even so, the 911 could only take Porsche so far. The decision to take on the EA425/ Porsche 924 project was the right one in the circumstances. Laying down a fresh design would have tied up years of development and demanded heavy financial commitment. A special production line at Neckarsulm was dedicated to Porsche for the manufacture of bodyshells. Apart from seating, only a sprinkling of components originated from Zuffenhausen. In design at least the 924, with its unusual transaxle transmission, was genuinely Porsche's own, with styling by Tony Lapine's department at Weissach. No cause for Porsche's loyal customers to complain. Or so you might have thought.

But there was considerable ambivalence. Porsche die-hards did not know quite what to make of the 924, talking in tragic tones about its 'van engine' which was anything but smooth at high revs, its four gappy gear ratios, its less than breathtaking brakes with drums at the rear, and occasionally intrusive noise levels. Some felt that the styling was somewhat effeminate, too, and those who thought their 924 was a passport to credibility in Porsche clubs around the world were sadly disillusioned.

More positively, if somewhat ironically, the 911 was making a concerted comeback during this time and continued to intrigue and excite Porsche customers. During 1976 Porsche's production breached the 20,000 barrier for the first time in the company's history. The total included 8,344 early production 924s most of which were placed in the German market, precisely 10,001 six-cylinder cars (7,313 of the 911, 1,531 Carreras

and 1,157 Turbos), and 2,000 examples of the temporarily revived four-cylinder 912 model, back in America for a year to plug the gap between the end of the 914/4 and the new 924. Porsche's overall profit improved by a factor of three that year, albeit only to DM7.4 million.

Derided as it was, the importance of the 924 to Porsche should not be underestimated. After all, it was responsible for introducing 100,000 new customers to the marque over a five-year period; people for whom Zuffenhausen's finest had been simply too expensive. Others were attracted by the pretty little coupé on its own merits and realistic price of DM24,000 (initially £7,000 in Britain). With back seats that folded flat to increase the luggage area, it was a surprisingly versatile and practical car, with overdriven gearing for economy and fine roadholding and cornering balance. Porsche had achieved all its design objectives while the transaxle transmission worked better than many had dared hope, clearly demonstrating the advantages of having equal front/rear weight distribution. And over the next few years, the 924 became slicker, quieter and generally more desirable.

It would have been a brave man to predict this level of success in 1975 when the 924 model was launched, involving the Stuttgart-Zuffenhausen firm in buy-out, and heavy development costs that could hardly be afforded as demand for the 911 was in one of its periodic depressions.

CHANGES AT PORSCHE

Until 1974, Dr Ing hc F. Porsche AG held a big, but exclusive, development contract with VW. Around 100 engineers were shifted from Zuffenhausen to the new Weissach facility in 1971 under the direction of Dipl Ing Ferdinand Piech. Basically, their job was to design and develop a replacement

Porsche's valuable research centre at Weissach includes a fast and demanding handling circuit.

for the Beetle. This was also a rear-engined model code-named (in VW's system) EA 266. Numerous prototypes were runners in 1971, powered by water-cooled overhead camshaft four-cylinder engines slung flat beneath the rear seats. It was no great secret that Porsche hoped to adapt the layout for a small sports car of its own. Another home-brewed Porsche enterprise at this time which did not make it through to the prototype phase, was a shortened, four-cylinder version of the 911 engine, perhaps to power this new sportscar.

VW was flat out to maintain its own solvency, however, and in September 1971 Rudolf Leiding supplanted Kurt Lotz as chief executive. As so often happens with a

new hand on the helm, sweeping changes were swiftly made: EA 266 development was ditched and the prototypes destroyed. As a sop he instigated the development of the EA 425, the intended successor to the VW–Porsche 914 model; being a joint off-shoot of both companies, based in Ludwigsburg but built by Karmann, it would cost VW very little and was of relatively minor importance.

Significant decisions were also taken in Zuffenhausen in 1971, though for entirely different reasons. Dr Ferdinand 'Ferry' Porsche had decided to strengthen and streamline his company, and as a first step he had what in government circles might be called a 'cabinet shake-up'. In short, members of the Porsche and cousin Piech families were

Ferdinand Piech

A year younger than brother 'Butzi', Ferdinand Piech was nicknamed 'Burli' or *little boy*. A talented and ambitious engineer who had started work, in 1963, on the development of the 911's flat-six engine and the five-speed transmission that eventually found its way into the 911, he abandoned his research and development post during the crisis of 1972 to go to a similar job at Audi. After sixteen years he was made chairman. Today, he is boss of the VW/Audi empire.

His influence at Audi was considerable, especially his unwavering support for the Quattro concept and full galvanized bodies. He believed that Audi lacked the strength of image to compete with Mercedes, BMW and Porsche but had few doubts that it would only be a matter of time before the marque acquired it.

Piech is a hard and capable driver and has used a Sport Quattro and a 300bhp Sport-engined 200 Quattro as personal transport. He likes to keep fit by jogging, skiing and cycling.

timeless 911 and Ferdinand developed its great flat-six; he also realized the potential of the awesome 917 racing cars. But there were too many squabbles. It was Dr Porsche's opinion that there were specks of sand in the well-oiled machine; good men were being held back.

In August 1972, the limited partnership KG (Kommanditgesellschaft) status was turned into joint stock AG (Aktiengesellschaft) status and the final phase of reorganization was concluded. Principal among the ten shareholders were Dr Ferdinand Porsche, his sister Louise Piech, each with four children having equal holdings.

One of Dr Fuhrmann's first jobs, in October 1971, was to establish the general design and configuration of the 928 model. He could not have known at the time that it wouldn't appear for nearly six years, its passage slowed by the oil crisis and consequent

Ferry Porsche

Son of Professor Ferdinand Porsche, the man responsible for the design of the VW Beetle, Ferdinand Alexander Porsche II, 'Ferry' is still the force behind the badge.

With guidance from his father, Ferry conceived the 911 and saw the 356 into existence. It was his desire that his eldest son, Butzi, should take over the family business but this led to a family rift and several younger members, including Ferdinand Piech, quit in 1972.

In the wake of the turbulence, Ferry Porsche hired Dr Ernst Fuhrmann as manager and gave him the unenviable task of finding a replacement for the 911. But as recent history illustrates all too clearly, it would not be that simple. Neither the 924 nor the 928 did anything to reduce demand for the rear-engined Porsche, even though nothing was done to the 911 to sharpen its appeal.

gently eased out. Dr Ernst Fuhrmann, the designer of the four-cam Carrera engine was appointed 'spokesman for the board' in the summer for 1971 and within twelve months the family members had gone. Ing Piech handed over the Weissach post to Dipl Ing Helmuth Bott, and Ferdinand 'Butzi' Porsche departed to form the independent – and highly successful – Porsche Design company in Austria. Second son Gerhard (Gerd) was a farmer with no active interest in the family business but the third son, Hans-Peter, decided to leave the production department, later joining Butzi at Porsche Design. The Porsche family had made a tremendous impact on Porsche cars. Butzi styled the

slump in business. An altogether larger car than the 911, it had a water-cooled engine at the front, trans-axle drive at the rear – the two connected by a rigid torque tube. The output target for its 4.7-litre V8 was 300bhp. Groomed as the 911's successor, it was anticipated that it might carry the major slice of responsibility for Porsche's success by 1984, the 911 having run its nominal twenty-year lifespan and finally been killed off by pollution regulations, noise control, crash safety and the like. Some prediction.

All this, of course, was closely linked with the EA 425 which permitted Porsche to develop the transaxle system on a small scale and sort out any teething problems with the implementation of the design. Starting a few weeks after project 928, the EA 425 began life as a VW. In 1974 came the slump which brought VW close to bankruptcy and turned EA 425 into a Porsche. All along, Rudolf Leiding had been as unenthusiastic about the VW–Porsche alliance in Ludwigsburg as Porsche itself. When he was forced to shed engineers in Wolfsburg, Porsche's deal to develop VWs was again thrown into the spotlight. The EA 425 sportscar was all that was left of the contract. This left VW–Porsche Vertriebsgesellschaft GmbH, headed by Otto-Erich Filius and K. Schneider, in an invidious position, since VW and Porsche each held a 50 per cent stake in a company that had been responsible both for developing and marketing.

VW–Porsche continued to sell the 914 and gear up for the launch of the EA 425 sportscar, though VW's own Scirocco coupé launched in March 1974 put a small spanner in the works by pre-empting the concept. It did not feel comfortable. So in the autumn of 1974 Dr Fuhrmann despatched VW–Porsche's sales manager, Lars-Roger Schmidt, to Leiding to suggest that Porsche should take on EA 425 and launch it as a Porsche. Schmidt was turned down.

But as bankruptcy closed in on VW,

Leiding was on the way out and in December he resigned on grounds of ill health. His replacement was Tony Schmucker and, in January 1975, Schmidt returned to Wolfsburg with his eyes on EA 425 and this time returned with the prize. It meant that EA 425 returned to Porsche lock, stock and barrel with Porsche paying a royalty on the first 100,000 cars built, rather than a lump sum. Nevertheless, Porsche still had to stump up DM100 million for the deal, which included buying out VW's half-share of the Ludwigsburg operation and the launch of the 924.

For VW it was an attractive deal. Without it Schmucker would certainly have wound up the former NSU plant at Neckarsulm, the least profitable of all VW's factories, where the Audi 100 and remains of the NSU RO80 were made. And it now meant that VW's Salzgitter plant could produce some 20,000 engines a year for the Porsche 924. Essentially these would be specially developed versions of the type 831 water-cooled four-cylinder unit, as used in the LT28 light van, and sold in short block form to American Motors for the Gremlin. With a 2-litre capacity and fuelled by Bosch K-Jetronic injection, the type 831 developed 125bhp in normally aspirated form. Neither was the 924 too proud to make extensive use of the VW–Audi parts bin: the four-speed manual or three-speed automatic transmission and steering, suspension and brakes all came from there. Even such things as instruments and door handles were VW, something of a throwback to the 356 sports car.

Schmidt was made sales director of Porsche in 1974, with the termination of VW–Porsche. Up to that point, he knew little about the 928. He is reported to have said that VW–Porsche was regarded as something of a nemesis by the Porsche family and deliberately kept in the dark. The bottom line was that Schmidt had the power of veto over the eight-cylinder model but in the end went along with Dr Fuhrmann, despite deep reservations.

THE TURNING POINT: THE LATE 1970s

The 928 was unveiled at the Geneva Show in March 1977 and precipitated a critical tidal wave of praise that carried it all the way to the international 'Car of the Year' title. Porsche's name was back in the bright lights and, in 1978, the 924 Turbo was launched with 170bhp, consolidating the idea that the company had the enthusiastic driver's best interests at heart.

Worldwide, the dealer network had clawed its way out of the 1974/75 doldrums and was expanding vigorously. In Britain sales exceeded 1,000 cars for the first time, more than half of them 924s. Whatever the initial misgivings, the 924 was turning out to be good news for the dealer network. Things were soon to look up in Japan, too. A year later Mitsuwa Motors in Tokyo also sold 1,000 Porsches for the first time. America still swallowed up the bulk of Porsche production, though – typically around 50 per cent. Of the remainder, 25–30 per cent would go to Germany and the rest shared out principally between Britain, France, Italy, Japan, Austria and Switzerland.

Back in Zuffenhausen, house-keeping was becoming a preoccupation. The old Second World War barrack buildings were in a poor state of repair and the 911s continued to be built in the same old labour-intensive way. The sheer intensity of decibels involved in panel beating was numbing, and in stark contrast to the relatively peaceful new 928 extension at Works II. Not that throughput was lax. On the contrary, twenty eight-cylinder cars could be made in each working day, a figure which suggested the 928 would indeed be the 911's successor by the mid-1980s with four cylinder models making up

the lower end. Who needed a 911 when a 944 Turbo was just as quick?

Well, Dr Porsche for one. For him and the quarter of a million who knew what it was to buy a new 911, there was no easy substitute; the six-cylinder car was unique. His instinct was that the 911 should continue in production for as long as demand for it existed. It proved to be the right one. Dr Fuhrmann's contention that the four and eight-cylinder models would elbow the 911 out of the frame had logical foundations but neglected to account for the emotional investments 911 customers had made in their favourite sportscar.

Perhaps unsurprisingly, relations between Dr Porsche and Dr Fuhrmann cooled, to the point where they avoided each other and weren't seen together in public. Dr Fuhrmann collected the Car of the Year award for the 928 from Prince Rainier in Monte Carlo by himself. The occasion turned out to be a double celebration, for the Almeras brothers' 911 had just won the Monte Carlo Rally, the fourth victory for the 911. The absent Dr Porsche would have approved.

Not all Porsche's sporting activities were going so well. At Le Mans, the Renault team comfortably despatched the Porsche factory's 936 team at its third attempt. Aware of the writing on the wall, investment in motor racing was cut right back. The intensively developed 935/78 raced only three times and its water-cooled four-valve-per-cylinder head technology was transferred to the 936 model. The race programme almost ground to a full stop after Porsche's Le Mans defeat in 1978. In the wake of that it was left to private teams such as Kremer Racing and Reinhold Joest to represent the Porsche name with the 935. Porsche entered Le Mans again in 1979 with a couple of Essex Petroleum-backed 936s but both retired, and the wet race went to a Kremer Porsche 935, the first time in many years that a production-based car had lifted the classic event.

The clash between Porsche's two prime movers had a certain inevitability. Dr Fuhrmann, by his own admission an engineer first and a marketeer last, went down with some style. In the summer of 1979, he dropped a hint to Dr Porsche that he would be leaving once a suitable successor had been located. And in 1979 he was awarded a Professor's seat at the University of Vienna – something of a last laugh.

In the summer of 1980, a replacement for Dr Fuhrmann was found – Peter Schutz, then a board member of the Klockner-Humboldt-Deutz (KHD) industrial plant and machinery company. Schutz's philosophy would be to expand the company, to prolong the career of the 911 and to invest substantially in research and production facilities; in fact to raise Porsche's game. He made significant changes in the boardroom

and wasted no time in hiring 'his own men'. Finance director, Heinz Branitzki stayed put and made a strong partner for research director Helmuth Bott, both of whom enjoyed Schutz's support. In 1981, however, Dr Heiko Lange was recruited from ITT to head the personnel department. And in January 1983 Professor Dr Rudi Noppen was brought in from KHD to direct the production and supply departments. The departure of Lars-Roger Schmidt from sales proved a problem in 1983, and it was nearly a year before a successor was named in Mario-Jon Nadelcu, but his tenure of office was short-lived: just a year.

THE STORM CLOUDS GATHER

On the face of it, Porsche had been doing well. Production to July 1979 hit a new high

Ernst Fuhrmann, Helmut Bott, Wolfgang Eyb (construction manager) and Wolfgang Mobius (body designer) pose with Porsche's 'Car of the Year'.

of 41,350 cars but, for the second year running, demand in America for the 924 had slumped, though offset partly by the strong demand for the 928. The Americans did not pull their punches over the 924, branding it a 'lemon', and US sales tumbled from 13,700 in 1977, to 8,400 in 1979 and to 5,400 in 1980. Sales of the 928 in 1978–80 were rosier, though, averaging 1,500 a year.

That said, the 924 had made its mark, reaching 100,000 sales in five years. Not bad at all when you consider it would make only 38,000 sales over the next five years once out of the American market. At this stage, remember, the 944 was still two years away. Porsche would have to face the depression on a downbeat. Unsurprisingly it was the American market that would inflict the most pain, the DM/Dollar ratio having fallen to an all-time low of 1.72. Porsche was left more bruised by the blow than either Mercedez-Benz or BMW.

Cost cutting was absolutely imperative. In 1980 production fell by a calamitous 25 per cent to 31,138, of which the Americans took fewer than 12,000, or 38 per cent. The US dealers, numbering around 350, had Porsches oozing out of the seams and each, on average, sold just 34 cars. It was not all doom and gloom, though. Britain bucked the trend, its 26 dealers selling a total of 2,000 cars, an average of 77 each – the stuff of good profits.

In truth, Porsche had an image problem in America. Imports were the responsibility of Audi–VW and Porsches were sold shoulder-to-shoulder with Audis and VWs. It made the Porsches look like up-market variants rather than independent quality products for discerning enthusiasts. On a 'bangs for bucks' basis, the 924 did not fare too well against cars like the VW Scirocco and the Mazda RX–7. Porsche's sales director Lars-Roger Schmidt embarked on a marketing mission to brush up the US image via the dealer network, a tactic whose effect would be felt on the other side of the recession. Between the bleak years of 1979 and 1982, however, its impact was limited.

When your back is against the wall, strict cost management is a more effective weapon. In 1980, Mr Bott was asked why gas struts were not fitted to the 924's bonnet. The answer was 24 Deutschmarks. Along the same lines, neither did the 924 have a remote release switch for the glass tailgate. The Mazda RX–7 did. Mazda outsold Porsche.

Pricing has always been a subject for debate within Porsche, the marketeers pulling one way and the engineers, keen to roll back technical frontiers, showing a healthy disregard for unit costs. When the Mark is steady or weak against foreign currencies, especially the dollar, the problem is less acute but it never goes away. And sometimes – as in 1974, 1980 and 1987 – it hurts.

Battles raged over the 928's pricing, as they did in 1981 when the 944 was nearing its launch. Peter Schutz wanted the 944 at an attractive 'introductory' price and proposed DM35,000. Finance director Heinz Branitzki felt the true sales price was DM42,000. In the event, the 944 went on sale at DM39,000, an artful compromise that pleased the boardroom and the dealer network. Pricing the 944 Turbo was even harder. Commercial good sense dictated that it should be 10 per cent cheaper than the 911 but the costings did not agree and put the price 10 per cent more expensive. The discrepancy was so serious that Schutz considered scrapping the model but was overruled. In the States it was priced halfway between the 944 and the 911, and while the dollar was strong, the sums worked out but when the exchange rate fell it became a big problem.

But Schutz soon started to work his magic. Within weeks of his appointment, the company had regained its sense of direction. In 1981 Porsche's performance was at rock bottom with production, in the 1981 model year to July, down to 28,015. America took fewer than 8,000 cars, the number of employees bottomed out at 4,900 and profits (not a reliable figure) levelled off at DM10million.

The rise in the value of the US dollar enjoyed by all the leading European exporting manufacturers would help Porsche recover. Its real saviour, though, was the 944. Within two years it reached and maintained a production level in excess of 50 per cent of Porsche's annual output. In the 1983 model year, the first full year of export to America, over 14,000 Porsche 944s crossed the Atlantic, and in the 1985 model year 944 production reached an all-time high of 27,460 units, easily exceeding the 924 in its best year.

The investment cycle had started again and, in June 1982, a new, fully computer-operated parts distribution warehouse was opened at Works II at a cost of DM50million. DM23million was invested in a new 'environment centre' at Weissach, the most advanced emissions laboratory in Europe, 50 per cent of whose capacity would be allocated to customer contracts. And in 1986 the much-needed new paint shop was opened at Works II (DM100million), and a few weeks later a new full-size wind tunnel was christened at Weissach, completing a further DM37million expenditure.

The revitalization at Weissach was clear for all to see: nearly 100 outside contracts, staff of 1,000 and turnover, at DM172million, that accounted for 13.9 per cent of the company's annual budget. Roughly 40 per cent of the work was for clients and consistently profitable. Today, that list includes SEAT (owned by VW) and Volvo. Both have cars with engines that have benefited from Porsche expertise.

On the competitions front, a new department was formed to prepare the 936 model for Le Mans, the only major change being the adoption of the old Can-Am four-speed gearbox which, although not fitted with suitable ratios, was rated to 1,000bhp and would be 100 per cent reliable. The 936, driven by Jacky Ickx and Derek Bell, won the 24-hour race with speed to spare. Shortly after that Schutz gave the green light to the development of the 956 model designed specifically for the new Group C formula to be introduced in 1982. It was more than a good move: it turned out to be the most successful race programme in Porsche's history. For all practical purposes, the 956 and its successor, the 962, were virtually unbeatable between 1982 and 1986.

A new competitions centre at Weissach, built away from the main block adjacent to the test track, was headed by Peter Falk, a senior member of the research department; it soon became known as 'Falkland'. Here was the space for ten engineers and thirty mechanics to express themselves. They formed the permanent staff engaged in the design, development, testing and race preparation of the factory's Group C cars, and the Formula 1 engines under contract to TAG and McLaren International.

In 1982 there was concerted recovery in all markets, both stimulated and exploited by the 944. Two hundred new jobs were created at Weissach, many in the new environment centre, and Porsche's payroll rose to 5,350. Turnover increased by 27 per cent to a record DM1,488million and profits by a factor of 3.7 to DM37.6million.

The 1982/83 financial and model years confirmed the upward trend, production rising by an unprecedented 38 per cent to 45,240 cars. Exports to America exceeded 20,000 cars for the first time since 1977 and profits improved by 85 per cent to DM69.6 million, although investments had risen to slightly over DM131million. In the first year of Schutz's appointment, investments had risen by 50 per cent from DM80million to DM125.7million.

The up-turn had many factors but capital

spending on buildings, equipment and the development of new models must all take part of the credit. In particular, the 911 Cabriolet was critically lauded, and everyone knew about the phenomenal 959 that would be unveiled at the Frankfurt Show in September, 1983 – the most technologically advanced road car of its time.

Production levels were pushed all round, extending the old-fashioned production lines to their limit and raising total capacity to 71 cars a day, the 911 lines producing 53 cars instead of 45, and the 928S line 21 instead of 18. The 4.5-litre 928 had been dropped as demand for the more powerful and much more expensive 4.7-litre 928S still outstripped supply. At Neckarsulm a double-shift was introduced to raise four-cylinder production from 72 to 130 cars per day, all but a handful the new 944 model as the 924 went into its final year.

In the 1983 model year, exports to America rose by 73 per cent to 20,235, but this was no more than 45.4 per cent of total production. The German domestic market accounted for 12,200 Porsches (27 per cent), Britain for 3,334 cars (7.2 per cent), France 2,106 cars (4.3 per cent) and Italy 1,400 cars (3.1 per cent).

By this time Schutz was on a roll and, at the start of 1983, he caused a sensation in America by announcing that Porsche's contract with Audi–VW, which expired in August 1984, would not be renewed. Instead, Porsche would set up its own distribution network, weeding out the weaker dealers and forming new ones in key areas. The dealer backlash was predictable but ineffectual.

So in September Porsche Cars North America was opened in Reno, Nevada, the Porsche company having a 96 per cent shareholding valued at DM65million. Canadian John Cook was appointed president of PCNA with 320 dealerships under his wing. No contracts were cancelled arbitrarily, all

writs were withdrawn, and the weaker dealers simply did not have their contracts renewed when they expired. American sales were now firmly in the ascendant, breaching 20,000, and the profits rolled in as each strong dollar bought DM3.4.

In competition, it was almost like old times. Victory for Rene Metge's 911/959 hybrid in the 1984 Paris–Dakar rally was repeated two years later, this time in a definitive 959, with a turbocharged engine, electronically split 4wd system and new six-speed gearbox.

On the race circuits in 1984 Niki Lauda and Alain Prost, in their TAG-powered Marlboro McLarens, were running away with the Drivers' and Constructors' Championships, scoring a total of 12 wins in 16 races. For many years, Porsche had dominated sportscar endurance events, sometimes against modest competition. Breaking into F1 and succeeding against manufacturers like Ferrari, Renault and Honda was something else.

In 1985 a double-shift system was introduced at Zuffenhausen to pump up production from 80 to 100 cars per day. Porsche's business was doing well in other parts of the world, too. At Calcot, Reading, Porsche Cars Great Britain Limited opened a large, hi-tech import centre valued at £11 million to handle 3,500 sales a year, employing around 200 staff. In America, PCNA sold 28,671 cars in the 1986 financial year, although the exchange rate was beginning to fall from its peaks and undermine profits, from an all-time high of DM120million to just DM75.3million.

Production of the 944 reached a record level at 27,460 in 1985 and there were two new versions waiting in the wings to enhance the model's reputation. The 944 Turbo, which was very nearly as rapid as the 911 Carrera, was launched in 1985 and the 16-valve 944S a year later, though this latter model, with higher performance than the

8-valve car noted particularly at the upper end of the power band, was not the runaway success Porsche had hoped for.

There was no ambiguity, though, about the appeal or sales potential of the 32-valve Porsche 928 S4. Smoother through the air and more powerful than its predecessor (320bhp), it became the fastest model in Porsche's range, even outstripping the 911 Turbo for top speed. Al Holbert, Porsche's motor sports director in America, drove the newcomer in virtually standard form at 171mph (275km/h) on the Bonneville salt flats. Impressively, his production car was equipped with full three-way catalytic equipment, underlining Porsche's stated policy of offering equal performance in all markets with new models.

Porsche was the first company to combine low emissions with high performance. A dark shadow had been cast over the 1983 Frankfurt Show by talk of German and European legislation calling for catalytic hardware. It looked ominously like the days of unrestricted high performance were numbered. Cars with emission equipment were fine for America, with its 55mph (88km/h) speed limit but would be slow, expensive and unreliable in European conditions, especially on the autobahns. Porsche proved the merchants of doom spectacularly wrong.

As for hardware, the future holds rear- and mid-engined cars with new water-cooled V6 and V8 units that were originally designed for the 989. Economies of scale have become such an important issue that Porsche can not forever afford the luxury of three different engine lines. All future Porsche powerplants will therefore share pistons, con-rods, valve gear and cylinderhead design. By using CNC (Computerized Numerically Controlled) tooling equipment, it may even be possible to create an all-new flat-six engine, but for the time being the emphasis clearly lies on the V6 and the V8. No similarities exist between these engines and the Audi sixes and eights, and the same applies to the drivetrain of the 989.

The 996 will replace the 30-year old 911 (by then, the facelifted 993) in 1996, powered by a choice of an all-new V8 engine or an up-dated version of the flat-six, mid-mounted. A year before the 996 will be the more affordable 986 (based on the Boxter showcar) at low cost.

Imminent at the time of writing is the 968 Cabrio Club Sport. Like the 1992 968 CS, the CS Cabrio has a stripped-out interior devoid of most of the standard car's electrical goodies and with lightweight seats. Gone, too, is the powered hood. This helps keep price as well as weight down. This car should make its début at Frankfurt in September.

Also destined for 1993 launch, the 968 Turbo S (or RS in racing trim) is powered by a twin-turbo version of the 968's 3-litre four-cylinder engine. This engine produces 337bhp in racing form and 305bhp at 5,600rpm for the road. Torque is phenomenal: the racing engine produces 369lb ft at 3,000 rpm. The car retains the 968's six-speed gearbox. The Turbo S is about 50kg lighter than the 968 Club Sport and, with a top speed in excess of 170mph (273km/h) and a 0–60mph (0–96km/h) time of under 5 seconds, probably the quickest front-engined Porsche ever made.

Appendix I

ROAD CARS

1977

Car: 924
Cylinders: 4-in-line
Capacity: 1,984cc
Bhp/rpm: 125/5,800
Length (in/mm): 166/4,216
Width (in/mm): 66/1676
Height (in/mm): 50/1,270
Wheelbase (in/mm): 94/2,388
Weight (lb/kg): 2,592/1,176

1978

Car: 928
Cylinders: V8
Capacity: 4,474cc
Bhp/rpm: 240/5,500
Length (in/mm): 176/4,470
Width (in/mm): 72/1,829
Height (in/mm): 50/1,270
Wheelbase (in/mm): 98/2,489
Weight (lb/kg): 3,151/1,429

1979

Car: 924 Turbo
Cylinders: 4-in-line
Capacity: 1,984cc
Bhp/rpm: 170/5,500
Length (in/mm): 166/4,216
Width (in/mm): 66/1,676
Height (in/mm): 50/1,270
Wheelbase (in/mm): 94.5/2,400
Weight (lb/kg): 2,601/1,180

1980

Car: 928S
Cylinders: V8
Capacity: 4,664cc
Bhp/rpm: 300/5,900
Length (in/mm): 176/4,470
Width (in/mm): 72/1,829
Height (in/mm): 50/1,270
Wheelbase (in/mm): 98/2,489
Weight (lb/kg): 3,198/1,451

1981

Car: 924 Carrera GT
Cylinders: 4-in-line
Capacity: 1,984cc
Bhp/rpm: 210/6,000
Length (in/mm): 166/4,216
Width (in/mm): 66/1,676
Height (in/mm): 50/1,270
Wheelbase (in/mm): 94.5/2,400
Weight (lb/kg): 2,650/1,202

1983

Car: 944
Cylinders: 4-in-line
Capacity: 2,479cc
Bhp/rpm: 163/5,800
Length (in/mm): 166/4,216
Width (in/mm): 68/1,727
Height (in/mm): 50/1,270
Wheelbase (in/mm): 94.5/2,400
Weight (lb/kg): 2,601/1,180

1983/84

Car: 928S
Cylinders: V8
Capacity: 4,664cc
Bhp/rpm: 310/5,900
Length (in/mm): 176/4,470
Width (in/mm): 72/1,829
Height (in/mm): 50/1,270
Wheelbase (in/mm): 98.4/2,499
Weight (lb/kg): 3,198/1,451

1985/86

Car: 924S
Cylinders: 4-in-line
Capacity: 2,479cc
Bhp/rpm: 150/5,800
Length (in/mm): 166/4,216
Width (in/mm): 66/1,676
Height (in/mm): 50/1,270
Wheelbase (in/mm): 94.5/2,400
Weight (lb/kg): 2,566/1,164

Car: 944 Turbo
Cylinders: 4-in-line
Capacity: 2,479cc
Bhp/rpm: 220/5,800
Length (in/mm): 166/4,216
Width (in/mm): 68/1,727
Height (in/mm): 50/1,270
Wheelbase (in/mm): 94.5/2,400
Weight (lb/kg): 2,774/1,258

Car: 928S–USA
Cylinders: V8
Capacity: 4,957cc
Bhp/rpm: 288/5,750
Length (in/mm): 176/4,470
Width (in/mm): 72/1,829
Height (in/mm): 50/1,270
Wheelbase (in/mm): 98.4/2,499
Weight (lb/kg): 3,418/1,550

1987/88

Car: 944S
Cylinders: 4-in-line, 4 valves per
cylinder
Capacity: 2,479cc
Bhp/rpm: 190/6,000
Length (in/mm): 166/4,216
Width (in/mm): 68/1,727
Height (in/mm): 50/1,270
Wheelbase (in/mm): 94.5/2,400
Weight (lb/kg): 2,722/1,235

Car: 924S
Cylinders: 4-in-line
Capacity: 2,479cc
Bhp/rpm: 160/5,900
Length (in/mm): 166/4,216
Width (in/mm): 66/1,676
Height (in/mm): 50/1,270
Wheelbase (in/mm): 94.5/2,400
Weight (lb/kg): 2,566/1,164

Car: 928S4
Cylinders: V8, 4 valves per
cylinder
Capacity: 4,957cc
Bhp/rpm: 320/6,000
Length (in/mm): 176/4,470
Width (in/mm): 72/1,829
Height (in/mm): 50/1,270
Wheelbase (in/mm): 98.4/2,499
Weight (lb/kg): 3,484/1,580

1989/90

Car: 944S2
Cylinders: 4-in-line, 4 valves
per cylinder
Capacity: 2,990cc
Bhp/rpm: 211/5,800
Length (in/mm): 166/4,216
Width (in/mm): 68/1,727
Height (in/mm): 50/1,270
Wheelbase (in/mm): 94.5/2,400
Weight (lb/kg): 2,955/1,340

Car: 944 Turbo
Cylinders: 4-in-line, 4 valves
per cylinder
Capacity: 2,479cc
Bhp/rpm: 250/6,000
Length (in/mm): 166/4,216
Width (in/mm): 68/1,727
Height (in/mm): 50/1,270
Wheelbase (in/mm): 94.5/2,400
Weight (lb/kg): 3,087/1,400

Car: 928GT
Cylinders: V8, 4 valves per
cylinder
Capacity: 4,957cc
Bhp/rpm: 330/6,200
Length (in/mm): 176/4,470
Width (in/mm): 72/1,829
Height (in/mm): 50/1,270
Wheelbase (in/mm): 98.4/2,499
Weight (lb/kg): 3,450/1,565

1991/92

Car: 968
Cylinders: 4-in-line, 4 valves
per cylinder
Capacity: 2,990cc
Bhp/rpm: 240/6,200
Length (in/mm): 166/4,216
Width (in/mm): 68/1,727
Height (in/mm): 50/1,270
Wheelbase (in/mm): 94.5/2,400
Weight (lb/kg): 2,650/1,202

Car: 928GTS
Cylinders: V8, 4 valves per
cylinder
Capacity: 5,397cc
Bhp/rpm: 350/5,700
Length (in/mm): 176/4,470
Width (in/mm): 72/1,829
Height (in/mm): 50/1,270
Wheelbase (in/mm): 98.4/2,499
Weight (lb/kg): 3,564/1,617

COMPETITION CARS

1980

Car: 924GTP
Cylinders: 4-in-line
Capacity: 1,984cc
Bhp/rpm: 320/7,000
Length (in/mm): 165/4,191
Width (in/mm): 73/1,854
Height (in/mm): 47/1,194
Wheelbase (in/mm): 94.5/2,400
Weight (lb/kg): 2,050/930

1981

Car: 924GTR
Cylinders: 4-in-line
Capacity: 1,984cc
Bhp/rpm: 375/6,400
Length (in/mm): 167/4,242
Width (in/mm): 73/1,854
Height (in/mm): 47/1,194
Wheelbase (in/mm): 94.5/2,400
Weight (lb/kg): 2,083/945

Car: 944GTP
Cylinders: 4-in-line
Capacity: 2,479cc
Bhp/rpm: 420/6,800
Length (in/mm): 167/4,242
Width (in/mm): 73/1,854
Height (in/mm): 47/1,194
Wheelbase (in/mm): 94.5/2,400
Weight (lb/kg): 2,183/990

1986

Car: 944 Turbo Cup
Cylinders: 4-in-line
Capacity: 2,479cc
Bhp/rpm: 220/5,800
Length (in/mm): 166/4,216
Width (in/mm): 68/1,727
Height (in/mm): 47/1,194
Wheelbase (in/mm): 94.5/2,400
Weight (lb/kg): 2,822/1,280

1987

Car: 944 Turbo Cup
Cylinders: 4-in-line, 4 valves per
cylinder
Capacity: 2,479cc
Bhp/rpm: 250/6,000
Length (in/mm): 166/4,216
Width (in/mm): 68/1,727
Height (in/mm): 47/1,194
Wheelbase (in/mm): 94.5/2,400
Weight (lb/kg): 2,876/1,304

Index